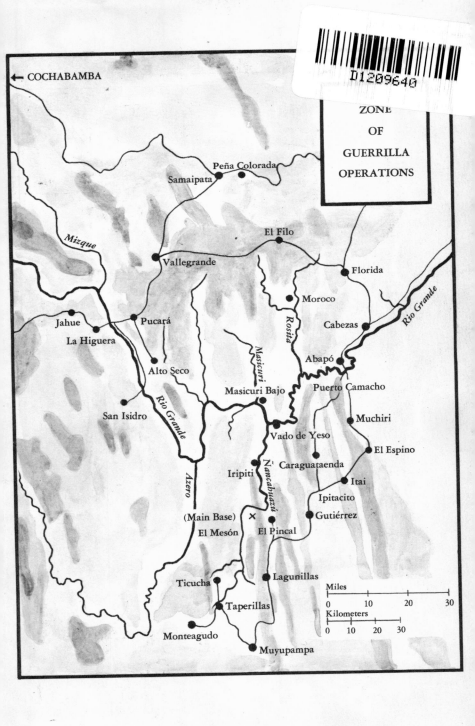

← COCHABAMBA

D1209640

ZONE
OF
GUERRILLA
OPERATIONS

Mizque

Peña Colorada
Samaipata

El Filo

Vallegrande

Florida

Moroco

Rosita

Rio Grande

Jahue
La Higuera

Pucará

Cabezas

Alto Seco

Masicuri

Abapó

Masicuri Bajo

Puerto Camacho

San Isidro

Rio Grande

Vado de Yeso

Muchiri

El Espino

Caraguataenda

Iripiti

Ñancahuazú

Itai

Ipitacito

Azero

(Main Base)
El Mesón

×

El Pincal

Gutiérrez

Ticucha

Lagunillas

Taperillas

Miles
0   10   20   30
Kilometers
0   10   20   30

Monteagudo

Muyupampa

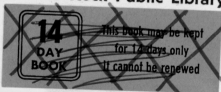

Death of a Revolutionary

Che Guevara's Last Mission

Death of a Revolutionary

Che Guevara's Last Mission

ᒍᒍᒍᒍᒍᒍᒍᒍᒍᒍᒍᒍᒍᒍᒍᒍᒍᒍᒍᒍᒍᒍ

RICHARD HARRIS

W · W · NORTON & COMPANY · INC ·

NEW YORK

FIRST EDITION

393   07445   5

Library of Congress Catalog Card No. 79-77405

Published simultaneously in Canada
by George J. McLeod Limited, Toronto

PRINTED IN THE UNITED STATES OF AMERICA
1 2 3 4 5 6 7 8 9 0

To young revolutionaries everywhere

Contents

Photographs between pages 94 and 95.

Preface

Any book written about such a controversial and popular figure as Che Guevara is an open invitation to all manner of criticism. If it pleases some it will surely anger others, and in all frankness this writer has sought to please no one, so the probability is great that this book will displease those who admire as well as those who abhor Che Guevara. This is, in the author's opinion, a regrettable but necessary consequence of any honest effort to provide an objective account of Che's fatal last mission. The author sincerely believes that only by reporting the facts of Che's Bolivian mission in an unbiased manner can true justice be done to his historical image and to the present status of the revolutionary struggle in Latin America.

The reader will find frequent quotes throughout this book taken from Che's Bolivian campaign diary as well as his previous writings. In every case these have been translated from Che's Spanish by the author himself, with the assistance of his Latin American friends. In general, they conform to the translations of Che's writings which have been published for commercial distribution. However, in certain cases, a different word or choice of phrasing has been used in order to convey the original meaning in the best possible manner. The version of Che's diary used throughout is that which was published by the Chilean magazine *Punto Final* and is the same as the version first made public by the Cuban government.

It is impossible to acknowledge all the help I have received in writing this book, but I should like to mention in particular Allen Stevenson, my Chilean-American research assistant, who accompanied me to Bolivia to help unravel the details of the story surrounding Che's guerrilla operation there. I also want to thank the Gills, who helped us in so many ways and made us feel at home while we were in Bolivia. Finally, I want to express my deep appreciation and gratitude to the many Bolivians who provided me with most of the information presented in the following pages of this book. Without their invaluable assistance, this book would not have been possible. It is my fervent hope that the future of their country will be one in which their hopes and aspirations will be fulfilled.

R. L. Harris
Santa Barbara,
August, 1969

"In the arduous profession of the revolutionary,
death is a frequent occurrence."

—Ernesto "Che" Guevara

Introduction

⎍⎍⎍⎍⎍⎍⎍⎍⎍⎍⎍⎍⎍⎍⎍⎍⎍⎍⎍⎍⎍⎍⎍

On October 10, 1967, the half-nude body of Ernesto "Che" Guevara was displayed to members of the international press in the
dusty little town of Vallegrande, Bolivia. Shot to death only a few
hours earlier, he looked remarkably alive. His eyes were open and
his lips were half parted in an expression that could be interpreted
as either a faint smile or a mocking sneer. As the photographs
of this haunting face and the news of the death of this famous revolutionary were spread around the world, people everywhere felt a
sense of shock and disbelief. The circumstances surrounding his
death were perplexing. It did not seem possible that a person of
his importance and capability could have been captured and killed
by the army of one of Latin America's weakest and poorest nations.

Since his death, Che Guevara has become one of the greatest legendary figures of our times. He is regarded as a popular hero
among the youth in every part of the world. His name, his ideas,
and his romantic image have become part of the symbolism of
those who believe that the injustices of this world can be erased
only by revolutionary means. Rarely in history has a single figure
been so passionately and universally accepted as the personification

of revolutionary idealism and practice. Moreover, even those who feel no sympathy for the ideals he upheld seem to be affected by the charisma of his almost mystical image.

Because he has become a popular myth and a revolutionary symbol, those who admire his example as well as those who abhor what he represents possess a greatly distorted conception of the man who was Che Guevara. Today, the growing number of articles, pamphlets, books, and films on Che picture him as a man who could never have breathed or walked on this earth. In the current literature on Che, his virtues tend to be magnified out of all proportion, his faults are glossed over, and his true personality is ignored. The real Che lies buried beneath the debris of propaganda and sensational journalism.

By impartially sifting and interpreting the facts available, this book seeks to rescue both Che's death and the circumstances surrounding the failure of his Bolivian mission from the clutches of the mythmakers, pamphleteers, and scriptwriters. It is based upon the assumption that behind every myth lies a reality far more fascinating and significant than that which the sensationalists and mythmakers conjure up.

To write about some aspect of human reality and to convey to others as clear a picture of it as possible requires a delicate balance between personal detachment and sensitivity. To remain objective and impartial in the analysis of human affairs is of course very difficult, but this does not mean we should abandon all such efforts. For this reason, this book seeks to provide an objective account of the last months of Che's life, without either justifying or condemning his beliefs and actions.

The objective interpretation of facts does provide a basis for drawing conclusions. Therefore, this book will be concerned with providing answers to such questions as: Did Che die a victim of his own tragic errors or of the treachery of Bolivia's Communists? Was he a great revolutionary or a psychopathic adventurer? Was his Bolivian operation a total failure or a partial success? Is it possible that he went to Bolivia with the knowledge that he would die there, or was he misled into thinking that his chances of victory were very good? The answers to these and other questions emerge from an objective analysis of the facts, and thus they have an important place in a book of this sort.

Thanks to the diary that Che kept during the period between his arrival in Bolivia and his capture some eleven months later, the author has had at his disposal a primary source of exact and detailed information concerning this final episode in Che's life. This unique source has made it possible to see Che's Bolivian mission, in a sense, through his own eyes. Che's diary has provided not only a precise description of the daily incidents in the life of his guerrilla force, but also a valuable insight into the faults, mistakes, and recriminations that are inevitable in such an undertaking.

All the information obtained by the author from personal interviews and field research in Bolivia has been carefully compared and checked against Che's diary, and the high degree of congruence between these two categories of information has convinced the author that the diary is an authentic and honest account of what occurred during the last eleven months of Che's life. However, it does not give us much insight into what took place outside the guerrilla force during this period. For this the author has had to rely upon his own sources of information. In certain cases, however, Che's diary provides information even on this subject.

The field research upon which this book is based was carried out in Bolivia not quite a year after Che's capture and death. At that time, the political ramifications of Che's tragic odyssey in Bolivia, in particular the uproar caused by the publication of his diary (clandestinely sent to Cuba by one of the top members of the Bolivian government), were still causing trouble for the Bolivian government and military. Consequently, it was not an easy task to conduct research on the guerrilla episode. Nearly all official doors were closed to the snooping *gringo* professor from California. Nevertheless, alternative sources of information were utilized, and several members of the Bolivian press, as well as the officials of certain left-wing political parties, proved to be extremely valuable informants.

Because the politically relevant stratum of Bolivian society is so small, approximately equivalent to the political elite of a medium-sized American city, access to a few key insiders means access to most of the country's political secrets. At any rate, in a small society like Bolivia, it is almost impossible to hide the truth about a subject as popular and fascinating as the death of Che Guevara. In fact, the real problem in this case was one of coping with the superabundance of information on certain aspects of this subject. The reader must judge whether the end result reflects the author's confidence that his research efforts turned up the essential facts.

Finally, the reader is encouraged to approach the subject of this book with compassionate objectivity. This is necessary because he is living in a world characterized by profound revolutionary ferment, although as an American he has had the good fortune to be raised in one of the most stable societies in all of man's history. For this reason, most Americans are out of touch with many of the aspirations and frustrations shared by the greater portion of humanity. And they are afraid of revolution at a time when it is the order of the day for millions around the globe, particularly in the developing areas of Latin America, Africa, and Asia. Thus, it is necessary to understand in objective terms why it is that most of the world is in revolution, and why other human beings choose to live and die as revolutionaries.

Death of a Revolutionary
Che Guevara's Last Mission

CHAPTER 1

Profile of a Revolutionary

⎍⎍⎍⎍⎍⎍⎍⎍⎍⎍⎍⎍⎍⎍⎍⎍⎍⎍⎍⎍⎍⎍⎍⎍

Revolutionaries are not born, they are made. Moreover, they do not spread revolution everywhere they go like the carriers of some infectious disease. Revolutionaries are molded by circumstances, societal conditions, and psychological factors. Unfortunately, the term "revolutionary" conjures up in the minds of many people a stereotype of a wild-eyed, bearded extremist who is driven by some fanatical urge to destroy the existing order of things, no matter what the cost in human life and property. On the other hand, certain revolutionaries, such as Che Guevara, capture the imagination and inspire others to create legends out of their lives. However, in order to understand why Che Guevara became a revolutionary and why he died as one, it is necessary to put aside any preconceptions one has about revolutionaries and look for the man behind the popular image. Only by knowing something about the man is it possible to gain greater insight into why he died such a tragic death in Bolivia.

Ernesto Guevara de la Serna was born on June 14, 1928, in the Argentine city of Rosario. His parents were of upper-class origin. His father was a contractor who had studied architecture but never received his degree. His mother was an intelligent and warm person who remained devoted to Ernesto, her first-born, until her death just a few years before his own. Soon after Ernesto was born, the Guevaras moved to San Isidro. It was in this city along the banks of the La Plata River that he contracted the illness from which he suffered for the rest of his life. His mother was an avid swimmer and used to take him with her to the yacht club in San Isidro when she went swimming. On one particularly chilly day, she had taken him with her, and by the time she was ready to leave the club she discovered he was very ill. She and her husband took him immediately to a doctor nearby, who informed them that their son had a severe asthmatic condition. For the next two years, Che's parents tried every possible cure, but in the end they were advised that they would have to move to a much drier climate if they wanted their son's health to improve. As a result, they moved to the little town of Alta Gracia in the central Argentine province of Cordoba.

Ernesto grew up in Alta Gracia, along with his two brothers and two sisters, who were born there. The dry climate of the region greatly benefited his health, although he continued to suffer periodic asthma attacks. As he grew older, Ernesto spent as much time outdoors as possible. His childhood friends recall that he was always organizing hikes to the hills and playing games requiring physical skill and endurance. His friends also remember him as a decisive and bold youth who was very sure of himself. But above all else, they remember him for his enthusiasm and adventurousness. Evidently, he was willing to do almost anything—perhaps to prove to himself and others that in spite of his chronic illness he was just as good as they. This personality trait stayed with him in later years. In fact, it appears to have been one of the most characteristic aspects of his adult personality.

Ernesto's family life was relatively happy. His father gave him considerable freedom, and his mother, who was never able to rid herself of the feeling that somehow she was at least partly responsible for his asthmatic condition, gave him a great deal of love and attention. Ernesto always confided in her, even years later when he became an important leader in the Cuban Revolution. Because of his asthma, he was often unable to attend school for days at a time during the first years of his primary education. Consequently, his mother helped him with his studies at home. Later on, when he entered secondary school, she taught him to speak French, although by this time the frequency of his asthmatic attacks had decreased considerably, and his attendance at school was quite regular.

Ernesto's parents wanted their children to be freethinkers. At home, the parents never spoke of religion, and the children were given considerable freedom to think and talk about all kinds of subjects. Ernesto's father felt strongly that the children should not be overprotected and that they should begin to learn life's secrets and dangers at an early age. When Ernesto was fourteen years old, his father let him take his brother, Roberto, on a hitchhiking trip to the surrounding provinces. They were gone almost the entire two months of their summer vacation, and Ernesto so thoroughly enjoyed himself on this trip that he became a determined hiker.

Despite his asthma, Ernesto played both soccer and rugby. In the former, he usually played the position of goalkeeper, always with an inhaler in his pocket. However, it was at rugby that he really excelled. His biographer, the Argentine writer Hugo Gambini, claims that the position Ernesto played in this game helped to define his personality. It seems he played "half-scrum," which is generally the key position in rugby since the majority of advances depend upon whoever is playing this position. Moreover, the player in this position is often the leader of his team, since he calls most of the plays and is the main ball-handler. Ernesto played this position as though both his personality and physical attributes had been made to order for it. Perhaps, as Gambini suggests, this game was instrumental in shaping Ernesto's personality as a daring leader.

All those who knew Ernesto as a youth were impressed by his

intelligence and the ease with which he learned new things. However, he was not an exceptional student, because his interests lay outside of school. He was preoccupied with hiking, football, rugby, and chess. The latter he learned to play at the age of eleven, and within a few years he was an excellent player. Later on, chess became his main hobby.

Ernesto grew up in a very politicized environment. Both his mother and father identified with the Republican cause during the Spanish Civil War, and after the war they became close friends with two Spanish families who had been forced to flee to Argentina when Franco came to power. Ernesto's family was also avidly anti-Nazi. His mother, in fact, formed a committee to send clothes and food to de Gaulle's Free French forces. She was a leftist and far more involved in politics than his father, who was a conservative. However, both of Che's parents militantly opposed Juan Perón's candidacy for the presidency of Argentina in 1946, and after Perón came to power, they joined the underground resistance movement against his regime.

Ernesto was eighteen when Perón came to power, and, like most other students his age, he was an anti-Peronist. However, he did not have much time to devote to political activities during this period. He had entered the Faculty of Medicine at the University of Buenos Aires and secured a job to pay for his expenses. What little spare time he had he devoted to rugby, chess, and travel.

At the beginning of 1950, Ernesto toured all of northern and central Argentina by motorbike—a trip of over thirty-five hundred miles. When he returned he took the motorbike back to the store where he had bought it in order to have it reconditioned. When the store owner discovered the details of the trip, he was astounded and asked Ernesto to give him a letter attesting to his having made such a fantastic trip by motorbike. This letter, along with a picture of Ernesto sitting on his motorbike, was published in a local sports magazine as an advertisement for the type of motorbike which he had used.

Ernesto's trip in 1950 served to whet his appetite for more travel and adventure. Exacty two years later, in 1952, when he lacked only one year of receiving his medical degree, he and a friend, Alberto Granados, a biochemist, set out to explore all of Latin America by motorcycle. This was a dream which they had nurtured while passing the weekends on short excursions and hikes in the mountains.

From Buenos Aires, Ernesto and Alberto went to the south of Argentina and crossed into Chile. As they neared Santiago, the motorcycle gave out and they were forced to continue on foot. They worked at various odd jobs in order to obtain money for their room and board. In this way, they managed to hitchhike their way across the extent of northern Chile to the Peruvian frontier.

In Peru, for the first time in their lives, they came in close contact with South America's suffering Indian masses. They saw how the Indians of the Peruvian *altiplano* (high plateau), whose ancestors were the great Incas, are exploited and brutalized by means of their addiction to *coca*. Because of Alberto's interest in leprosy, they visited a leprosarium on the banks of one of the tributaries of the Amazon river at San Pablo, Peru. There they worked in the leprosarium's laboratory and endeared themselves to the inmates. They played soccer with them, took them on hikes, and even led them on hunting expeditions. When it came time for Ernesto and Alberto to leave, the inmates gave them a very emotional farewell party.

From San Pablo, Ernesto and Alberto crossed the river to Leticia, Colombia, on a raft built for them by the inmates of the leprosarium. In Leticia, they managed to obtain free passage on a flight to Bogotá by playing for the town's football team. At the time, Colombia was under the dictatorship of Laureano Gómez, and all foreigners entering the capital were regarded by the authorities as potential subversive agents. When Ernesto and Alberto arrived in Bogotá looking like two expeditionaries, they were arrested and interrogated by the police. Indignant, they reacted angrily towards their captors, which only made their situation worse. A local student group heard of their plight and convinced the authorities that they should be released and allowed to leave the country.

From these students, Ernesto and Alberto learned that one of the agents they had berated had a reputation for having killed a number of people in Bogotá with less provocation than they themselves had given him. With this information and the financial assistance of the Colombian students, the two harassed travellers left Bogotá on a bus to Venezuela.

In Caracas, Venezuela, they met a doctor who was a specialist in leprology. Impressed by Alberto's interest in leprosy, he offered him a position in his laboratory at a hospital for lepers. At about the same time, Ernesto ran into a friend of his family who had an airplane which he used to transport racing horses between Buenos Aires and Miami. He told Ernesto that he could return with him to Buenos Aires if he wanted to resume his studies at medical school. Ernesto and Alberto made a pact: Alberto would accept the job offered him and stay in Venezuela, while Ernesto would go to Buenos Aires to graduate from medical school and then return to Venezuela to work with Alberto. It was the end of July, 1952, when they said good-by in Caracas.

When Ernesto left Caracas, the plane went to Miami before returning to Buenos Aires. Since the plane had to lay over for a couple of days in Miami, he took advantage of the opportunity to visit the city. There he ran into a boyhood friend who was studying at the University of Miami, and, instead of leaving in a few days, he decided to stay until the plane returned a month later. But he missed the plane when it returned, and he was repatriated to Argentina at the expense of the U.S. Department of Immigration.

After he returned to Argentina, Ernesto undertook a crash program to complete the requirements for his graduation from medical school. He met all the remaining requirements in less than a year, and obtained his medical degree in March, 1953. Since he did not have the money to go directly to Venezuela and join Alberto, he decided to travel to Venezuela in the same romantic manner that he and Alberto had reached there a year before. He used what little money he had to buy a train ticket from Buenos Aires to La Paz, Bolivia. He figured he would travel from Bolivia to Venezuela as best he could.

In July, 1953, Ernesto and his friend Carlos Ferrer took the three-thousand-mile train trip from Buenos Aires to La Paz. They arrived in the Bolivian capital a year after the country had undergone a dramatic popular revolution in which the major foreign-owned mines had been nationalized and the peasants had taken possession of the feudal estates on which they had formerly labored as serfs and tenant farmers. Thus, they found La Paz filled with an atmosphere of revolutionary fervor and excitement.

Soon after their arrival, Ernesto and Carlos met a group of Argentine exiles who had been forced to leave Argentina because of their opposition to the Perón regime. One of these exiles was a young lawyer named Ricardo Rojo. In a short time, Rojo and Ernesto became good friends and traveling companions. Since Che Guevara's death, Rojo has written about his long friendship with him and the experiences they had together in Bolivia and elsewhere in Latin America. Rojo recalls that when he met Ernesto in La Paz, he was living in a miserable rented room in one of the oldest parts of the city. Ernesto spent most of his time visiting ancient Inca ruins or passing the day in the noisy cafes along the capital's main boulevard, Avenida 16 de Julio. From these cafes, Ernesto, Rojo, and the others were able to look out on the broad and sunny boulevard and watch the continuous parade of the Bolivian people as they stopped to look at the large signs propagandizing the revolutionary goals of the new regime.

Rojo remembers that Ernesto expressed little interest in politics at the time and that he was pessimistic about the fate of the Bolivian revolution. He regarded the new regime as merely reformist and not truly revolutionary. On one occasion, Ernesto and Rojo visited the Ministry of Peasant Affairs, where they saw long lines of peasants being methodically sprayed with DDT. Ernesto reportedly was incensed by the humiliating way these peasants were being treated by a regime which claimed to be the instrument of their interests. According to Ernesto, the new regime was not solving the causes of Bolivia's problems but merely trying to ameliorate their effects. In the case of the peasants, the government was spraying them to rid them of lice, rather than trying to improve the social and economic conditions which were the cause of their lice.

During this period, Ernesto was neither a Marxist nor a revolutionary. He was definitely a noncomformist with a keen sense of social justice, but these traits had as yet not led him to espouse any particular political cause or ideology. Rojo recalls that when they first met, Ernesto was uncertain about what he wanted to do with his life, but very sure about what he did not want to do with it.

In September, 1953, Ernesto, Carlos, and Rojo left Bolivia for Peru. According to Rojo, Ernesto demanded that his traveling companions be willing to walk interminably, be devoid of any concern for the condition of their clothing, and accept without anguish the state of being absolutely without money. Soon after they entered Peru, they separated. Ernesto and Carlos went to visit Machu Pichu, and Rojo went on to Lima. A few weeks later, they met again in Lima, and from there they traveled together to Guayaquil, Ecuador. After several weeks in Guayaquil, Ernesto decided to accompany Rojo to Guatemala instead of going to Venezuela to join Alberto Granados. His decision appears to have been based on two considerations. First, he seems to have been influenced by Rojo's enthusiasm to observe at first hand the revolutionary regime then in power in Guatemala. But even more important probably was the fact that he had no money to travel any further, and Rojo had managed through friends in Guayaquil to obtain free passage for the two of them on a ship owned by the United Fruit Company that was bound for Panama.

Ernesto and Rojo didn't reach Guatemala until January, 1954, having spent a number of weeks on the way in Panama and Costa Rica. When they finally arrived in Guatemala City, they located themselves in a *pensión* where a number of young Peruvian exiles were staying. These Peruvians were militant members of Peru's left-wing APRA party, then under attack in Peru because of its opposition to the Manuel Odria regime. Offered asylum by the Guatemalan authorities, these Peruvians had found employment in the various agencies of the Guatemalan government which were engaged in economic planning and agrarian reform, subjects on which they were regarded as experts. Through their association with the Peruvians staying at their *pensión*, Ernesto and Rojo were introduced to a number of interesting people, both Guatemalans and exiles. Among these was a very attractive young Peruvian exile named Hilda Gadea.

Since Ernesto needed money to pay his bills at the *pensión* and wanted to stay in Guatemala, he went to the Ministry of Public Health to seek employment as a doctor in one of the government's public assistance programs. He was interested in working with one program in particular, which was being carried out among the Mayan Indians in the region of the ancient temple of Tikal. Rojo accompanied Ernesto when he went to see the minister of health about a position in this program. He recalls that everything went fine until the minister asked Ernesto whether he had a membership card in the *Partido Guatemalteco del Trabajo* (the name of the Guatemalan Communist Party). When Ernesto answered that he was not affiliated with the party but that he supported the revolutionary ideals of the Guatemalan regime, the minister indicated that without a party card there was nothing he could do for him. According to Rojo, Ernesto told the minister that the day he decided to affiliate himself with a particular political party it would be out of conviction and not out of necessity.

Having failed to secure employment as a doctor, Ernesto started selling encyclopedias. Before long, however, Hilda was able to obtain a position for him in one of the agrarian reform programs. Through Hilda, he became friends with a number of Guatemalan leftists, and at their suggestion he began to read the works of Marx and Lenin. From this point forward, he seems to have begun to take a serious interest in politics.

At the end of February, 1954, Ricardo Rojo received some money from his parents in Argentina, and he decided to travel to the United States. Ernesto chose to remain in Guatemala City because of his interest in Hilda and the revolutionary programs of the Guatemalan regime. But the turn of events soon brought his stay to an abrupt conclusion.

Before 1944, Guatemala had been just another "banana republic" ruled by a series of dictators who served the interests of the local oligarchy and the American-owned United Fruit Company. But in 1944, the ruling strong man, Jorge Ubico, was overthrown by a popular revolt led by junior army officers and students. On the surface, the revolt appeared to be aimed primarily at discarding Ubico's oppressive regime in favor of more democratic rule. But in reality, the groups who participated in the revolt demanded the complete reform of Guatemala's feudal economic and social order. Following the overthrow of the Ubico regime, elections were held and Juan José Arévalo became Guatemala's first elected president. Under Arévalo's rule a major effort was made to bring Guatemala's large Indian population into the twentieth century and a large number of farm and city workers were unionized. The revolutionary policies of Arévalo's regime were continued and in fact accelerated by Arévalo's successor, Jacobo Arbenz, who was elected to the presidency in 1951. By the time Ernesto and Rojo arrived in Guatemala, in early 1954, the Arbenz regime had distributed to some one hundred thousand Guatemalan peasants uncultivated land which the government had expropriated from the country's large feudal estates, including eleven thousand hectares of uncultivated land belonging to the United Fruit Company. The response from the U.S. was almost immediate.

At the March, 1954, foreign ministers' meeting of the Organization of American States, U.S. Secretary of State John Foster Dulles accused the Arbenz regime of being "Communist-infiltrated." He also succeeded in having passed the famous Resolution 93, which indirectly condemned Guatemala and expressed the right of the OAS members "to take the necessary measures to protect themselves against Communist intervention." The necessary measures in the case of Guatemala involved the preparation of a mercenary invasion force in neighboring Honduras and El Salvador. On June 17, this force, under the command of Carlos Castillo Armas, crossed the frontiers of Guatemala and began marching toward the capital. The invasion was supported by the CIA, who supplied the invaders with arms and planes and also arranged for the betrayal of the higher echelons of the Guatemalan army. In a matter of days the Arbenz regime collapsed and Castillo Armas assumed control of the country. One of his first acts was the issuance of a decree returning expropriated lands to their former owners.

When the invasion began, Ernesto and his Peruvian friends watched in exasperation as Arbenz naively relied upon the army to repulse the attack and refused to give arms to the various left-wing parties and organizations that were demanding them so that they could help defend "their revolution." As Castillo Armas' small force of mercenaries neared the capital with hardly any resistance from the army, Ernesto could no longer contain his frustration with what he saw happening around him. In a desperate effort to save the revolution which he had only recently adopted, he went to the leaders of the various left-wing youth organizations and exhorted them to assume immediate control of the capital and defend it against the mercenaries who were advancing against it. However, his frantic efforts to mobilize popular support for the Arbenz regime succeeded only in drawing the attention of the CIA and Castillo Armas' agents in the capital.

Ernesto would almost certainly have been imprisoned, and probably executed, if it had not been for the Argentine ambassador. Having been advised that there was an Argentine on the list of those who would be executed by the new regime, the ambassador went to Ernesto and offered him asylum in the Argentine embassy. At first Ernesto refused, but the ambassador convinced him that he couldn't do alone what the Guatemalans themselves were not disposed to do.

Ernesto remained approximately a month in the Argentine embassy in Guatemala City along with a number of other Latin Americans who were given asylum there. For the purposes of quartering these individuals, the embassy classified them either as "Communists" or "moderates." Because of his activities during the invasion, Ernesto was classified as a Communist and located in a special part of the embassy. Later, the ambassador offered him space on an Argentine military plane if he wanted to return to Argentina, but he declined the offer and asked the ambassador whether he could secure a guarantee of safe conduct for him so that he could travel to Mexico. This was arranged, and he departed by train for Mexico City, where Hilda and many of her Peruvian friends had fled several weeks earlier.

When Ernesto arrived in Mexico City, he discovered that it was a haven for exiles from all over Latin America. In addition to the latest influx of Guatemalan exiles, there were political refugees from the Dominican Republic, Peru, Cuba, Colombia, Venezuela, Haiti, and his own Argentina. Most of these exiles lived in the same *pensions* and frequented the same bars and cafes. Ernesto immediately located Hilda and together they rented a flat in the section of the city where most of the exiles were living. Shortly afterwards they were married, and in February, 1955, they had their first child, a girl.

Ernesto managed to make ends meet by taking pictures of the American tourists as a street photographer. He became a regular member of the exile community and was friendly in particular with the Cuban element. As time went by, he became increasingly bitter about his Guatemalan experience and developed a deep hatred for the United States, which he blamed for the overthrow of the Guatemalan regime and for most of Latin America's economic and political ills.

In one of the many gatherings of his fellow exiles, Ernesto met Raul Castro, Fidel's brother. The two Castro brothers had arrived in Mexico in mid-1955, following their release from a Cuban prison, where they had been incarcerated for the abortive attack they had led against the Moncada barracks in 1953. Ernesto was impressed by Raul's intelligence and his determination to return to Cuba and fight for the liberation of his people from Juan Batista and the *yanquis*. Through Raul, he met Fidel. They immediately took a liking to each other and became close friends. Fidel and Raul told Ernesto of their plans to invade Cuba with a contingent of well-armed men and appeal to the peasants to join them in revolting against the dictorial Batista regime. Ernesto asked if they could use a doctor in the contingent, and when they said yes, he volunteered to join them. Hilda recalls that from this point on, Ernesto spoke of nothing but the Cuban Revolution, and that in the end she lost her husband to this cause.

Fidel left Mexico for a time to seek support from the Cubans living in the United States who were opposed to Batista. From these fellow exiles he collected funds and recruits for his planned invasion, and when he returned to Mexico he obtained the services of a Colonel Alberto Bayo to train his recruits in the tactics of guerrilla warfare. Colonel Bayo, a former officer in the Spanish Republican Army, had gained a great deal of experience in guerrilla warfare in Morocco against the Arabs and in the Spanish Civil War against Franco's forces. With his assistance, Fidel established a secret training camp for his group at a large ranch in the mountainous Chalco district of Mexico. Fidel brought eighty men to the training camp, including Ernesto. At the end of the training period, Coronel Bayo singled out Ernesto as his best student.

It was during this training period in Mexico that Ernesto's Cuban comrades gave him the nickname "Che." They called him Che because like most Argentines he used the word *che* (similar to "Hey, man") in almost every sentence. He accepted this nickname with pride because it marked him as Argentine.

In November, 1956, Che and the others departed for Cuba on an old launch named *Granma*. Due to the poor condition of the boat, which was designed to carry twenty persons instead of over eighty, and the bad weather at sea, it took them a week to reach Cuban waters. When they finally reached the Cuban coastline near Cape Cruz, it was dark, and the launch got stuck in a marsh along the shoreline. As a result, the guerrillas were forced to abandon their heavy equipment and most of their supplies and make their way to dry land by wading through the muddy marsh. For several days they marched towards the neighboring Sierra Maestra without encountering any resistance, but on December 5, they were surprised by the army on a sugar cane plantation where they had stopped to rest. Only Che, Fidel, Raul, and nine others managed to escape and make their way to the Sierra Maestra. In the fighting Che was wounded in both the throat and chest, but his wounds were not serious and he survived with only the most rudimentary medical treatment.

The twelve survivors of the *Granma* were joined by five discontented peasants in January, 1957, and this miniscule group began operating as a guerrilla force from its hiding places in the Sierra Maestra. As the months went by, the guerrillas managed to carry out a number of daring attacks against small military outposts in the region, and the news of their actions attracted the support of student groups all over the country. In time, the ranks of the guerrilla force began to swell with recruits from these groups and from the sympathetic peasantry.

Che was to have been the medical officer of the force, but his value as a guerrilla leader soon became evident. He so distinguished himself in the group's first encounters with the army that Fidel gave him increasingly greater military responsibilities. In March, 1957, Fidel appointed him, along with Ramiro Valdes, Ciro Redondo, and Camilo Cienfuegos, to the rank of captain. A short time later, Che was promoted to the rank of *comandante* (major), the highest rank in the guerrilla army, and in July, 1957, Fidel placed Che at the head of a new column with instructions to operate apart from the main force.

By March, 1958, the guerrillas had succeeded in defeating every effort by the regular army to dislodge them from the Sierra Maestra. Consequently, Fidel decided to extend the scope of the war and sent his brother Raul to the northern end of Cuba's Oriente province to establish a second guerrilla front in the mountains there. At the beginning of April, he also called on the Cuban people to support a general strike against the Batista regime. But his call for a strike did not receive widespread popular support and Batista decided the moment had arrived to launch an all-out attack against Castro. He threw the full weight of the Cuban army, air force, and navy against the guerrillas. This massive offensive forced the guerrillas to give up 90 per cent of the territory over which they exercised some control. However, the offensive failed to destroy Fidel's rebel army, and by July, 1958, his men began to take the initiative away from Batista's troops. In fact, during the first eleven days of combat in July, the guerrillas captured over two hundred of Batista's soldiers, who were no match for Fidel's men in the rugged terrain of the Sierra Maestra.

Having turned Batista's offensive into a guerrilla victory, Fidel attracted major political support. On July 20, the leaders of the various Cuban political parties opposing the Batista regime, both moderates and conservatives, signed a declaration in Caracas in which they threw their support behind the guerrillas. The only party which refused to sign the Caracas Declaration was the Cuban Communist Party.

In August, 1958, Fidel gave Che instructions to take his column down from the Sierra Maestra toward the Province of Las Villas in the central portion of the island. As his column moved across the lowlands toward Las Villas, it won one battle after another, and the almost suicidal character of its maneuvers began to seriously demoralize the regular army. In a desperate attempt to shore up his shaky regime, Batista tried to stage a rigged national election in November, 1958. But the election was boycotted by a majority of the citizenry and by all the political parties which had signed the Caracas Declaration.

The public's repudiation of the election so infuriated Batista that he launched a reign of police terror against the general populace. The guerrillas took this as the cue to begin their general offensive. Fidel ordered Camilo Cienfuegos to take a column down to the plains and support Che in his drive toward Las Villas. From there, the two columns proceeded to cut the country in half and liquidate Batista's main forces in the eastern half of the island.

The decisive battle of the war was fought by Che's column in the city of Santa Clara on December, 1958. He arrived at the city at the head of a convoy of confiscated trucks and jeeps, which were filled with his guerrillas from the Sierra Maestra, as well as students and peasants who had joined his force in increasing numbers as he moved across the plains. The column moved first to the university, and from there Che sent contingents to capture various strategic points in the city. It was at this point that an armored train arrived in the city with four hundred reinforcements. Che gave his men instructions to concentrate their fire on the train when it stopped to unload its cargo of troops. As a result, the soldiers could not disembark. Moreover, when the train tried to reverse its direction, it was derailed; Che had ordered a patrol to separate the rails behind it after it arrived. Surrounded, and with no hope of escape, the soldiers had no choice but to surrender to the rebels.

As word went through the city of the capture of the reinforcements, the citizenry began barricading the streets with cars and buses in order to obstruct the movement of the army's tanks and armored cars. Then, from the balconies of their houses and apartments, the city's inhabitants and the guerrillas began throwing Molotov cocktails on the military vehicles as they attempted to pass through the barricaded streets. Batista ordered his air force to bomb the city, but, although many sections were reduced to rubble, the situation could not be reversed. Che's column had gained control of the city. On January 1, 1959, word reached Santa Clara that Batista and his immediate family had fled to the Dominican Republic. Informed of this, the troops still holding out in certain parts of the city surrendered to Che.

On January 3, 1959, Che and Camilo Cienfuegos arrived with their men in Havana. Meanwhile Fidel marched with his troops to Santiago de Cuba to capture the Moncada, the same fortress where he had made an abortive attempt six years earlier to bring down the Batista regime. On January 5, five Latin American countries recognized Fidel's provisional government. Great Britain and a number of other nations followed. On January 7, the United States recognized the new regime, and recalled Ambassador Earl Smith, who was unanimously condemned by Cuban public opinion for having supported Batista. Finally, on January 8, Fidel arrived in Havana, where Che and Camilo Cienfueges awaited him.

As Fidel triumphantly rode into the city, his brother Raul was at his right and Che was at his left. In less than three years, the young Argentine had risen from the obscure existence of a roving young adventurer to become one of the most popular and important leaders in the Cuban Revolution. Three years earlier he had only begun to think seriously about his political convictions and commitments, but now, at the age of thirty-one, he found himself an accomplished military commander and one of the three most powerful leaders in the new government of Cuba.

While historical circumstance, destiny, or fate—call it what you will—must be given some of the credit for Che's meteoric rise to fame and power, the importance of the man's personality must not be underrated. He seems to have possessed all the characteristics of the true believer and the charismatic leader. He had an amazing capacity for personal sacrifice, and he never compromised his ideals. From the time he became a guerrilla, he appears to have lived according to the motto *todo o nada* (all or nothing). In fact, he was so demanding of himself that he did not permit himself a single indulgence. This, of course, made it possible for him to demand a great deal from those around him.

Che had that quality of personal magnetism that attracts and inspires the loyalty and devotion of others. In the Sierra Maestra, his boldness and determination invoked the enthusiasm of his comrades, and it soon became clear to Fidel that Che was a natural leader. Once having elevated him to a position of leadership, Fidel found that Che was an extremely capable and resourceful military commander. He gave Che increasingly greater responsibilities, and in the end entrusted him with the most important and crucial campaign of the Cuban revolutionary war.

Fidel had complete confidence in Che, since he knew that Che had no personal political ambitions. He recognized that Che, as an Argentine, felt it was not his place to question the basic political objectives chosen by his Cuban comrades. Fidel knew that he could count on Che's loyalty and unquestioning devotion to the goals of the revolution. Their relationship was close, largely because of the similarity of their thinking, and it was only much later that Che ever differed with Fidel on any major issues.

After Fidel's seizure of power, there followed a period in which the new regime suffered a series of strains and internal struggles. On May 17, 1959, Fidel put into effect a new agrarian reform law which eliminated Cuba's large estates and turned their lands over to the formerly landless peasantry through a form of collective ownership. This was immediately interpreted by the press and government officials in the United States as a threat to private property. In the months that followed, the value of shares in Cuban sugar companies dropped to an all-time low on the New York Stock Exchange, and Cuba's relations with the U.S. government rapidly deteriorated.

During the first six months of the new government, Che became one of Fidel's closest confidantes and advisers. In February, 1959, Che was proclaimed by an official decree to be a Cuban by birth. He brought his first wife and their child to Cuba; subsequently, he obtained a divorce. On June 2, he married Aleida March, a Cuban secretary who had joined his guerrilla column six months before the end of the war. Less than two weeks after his marriage, the first serious crisis of the new Cuban government occurred, and five cabinet ministers who disagreed with Fidel over the direction the new regime should take, resigned. A few days later, Che left Cuba on a goodwill tour to Yugoslavia, the Middle East, and Asia. His departure was the result of pressure brought to bear on Fidel by those in the government who considered Che too radical.

Che returned to Cuba in September, 1959, after an absence of three months. In the meantime, Fidel had purged his government of the more moderate elements and had decided to sell 330 million tons of sugar to the Soviet Union. Shortly after Che's return, Fidel presided over a meeting of the new National Institute of Agrarian Reform and announced that he was appointing Che as head of the Department of Industries in that organization (later Che was made Minister of Industries and was given control over Cuba's agrarian reform and industrialization programs). At the end of November, Fidel appointed Che to the important post of president of the National Bank of Cuba, which placed him in charge of all the country's financial affairs. Shortly after Che assumed this position, he made a public declaration in which he indicated that Cuba would not give any special guarantees to foreign capital and that the country would seek trade and financial ties with the Communist bloc.

Throughout the early sixties, Che remained one of Fidel's closest advisers and one of the most important members of his cabinet. He was second only to Raul Castro in his proximity to Fidel. In addition to his political responsibilities, he wrote what has now become a classic work on guerrilla warfare, *La Guerra de Guerrillas*, plus several articles on various subjects, perhaps one of the most important being his "Notes for the Study of the Ideology of the Cuban Revolution."

To most of those who knew and observed him during the years he served at Fidel's side, Che was the model revolutionary leader. He was dedicated to his duties, absolutely convinced of the rightness of his cause, and devoted to Fidel. In the opinion of many, he was the most intelligent and persuasive member of Fidel's cabinet. But he was dissatisfied with the routine and bureaucratic aspects of his ministerial responsibilities. On a number of occasions he told his friends of his desire to return to the revolutionary struggle. As time went by, he spoke increasingly of the possibility of leaving his ministerial post and devoting his future efforts to the revolution against imperialism in Latin America and in other parts of the world.

In the fall of 1960, Che was asked by a reporter from *Look* magazine if he was an orthodox Communist. His answer was no, that he preferred to call himself a "pragmatic revolutionary." In fact, he was neither a pragmatic revolutionary nor an orthodox Communist. To be sure, his outlook, his prejudices, and the events in which he participated located him among the Communist ranks. But, as *New York Times* correspondent Herbert Matthews said after interviewing him in 1960, Che would have had no emotional or intellectual problem in opposing the Communists if the circumstances had been otherwise. He made common cause with the Communists because they were opposed to the same things in contemporary Latin American society that he was opposed to. Che differed from the orthodox Communists in that he refused to accept their rigid ideological interpretations of Latin

American society. He firmly believed that the Cuban experience demonstrated that socialist revolutions in the underdeveloped world could be successfully launched without the direction and control of an orthodox Communist party, and it was "heretical" views such as this which earned him the disfavor of the pro-Moscow Communists. On the other hand, his all-or-nothing mentality and his uncompromising devotion to the goal of extending the Cuban revolution to all of Latin America prevented him from being truly pragmatic.

Che's unorthodox views and his distrust of the Soviet Union made him the prime target of the pro-Moscow Communists in Cuba. The leader of this group, Anibal Escalante, finally succeeded in pressuring Fidel to accept Che's resignation from the cabinet in 1965. Some insight into this internal struggle was revealed in a letter which Escalante wrote to a member of the Central Committee of the Communist Party of Czechoslovakia in January, 1966. In this letter, a copy of which was obtained by a Cuban exile group in New York City, Escalante alleged that Che had suffered "mental aberrations and hallucinations" following his trip abroad during late 1964 and early 1965. He referred to Che's confinement in a mental hospital outside of Havana after his return and to his grandiose dreams about exporting his theories and techniques of guerrilla warfare to other countries and continents. According to Escalante, Cuba's economic instability and her strained relations with the Soviet Union were a direct result of Che's impractical projects and pathological adventurism.

Escalante's assertion that Che was mentally deranged must be discounted as an obvious attempt on his part to discredit a man who stood in the way of the policies advocated by Cuba's pro-Moscow Communists. Nevertheless, there is an element of truth in Escalante's letter. Che was a dreamer and an adventurer.

He was prone to dreaming up grandiose plans and projects, especially when he was confined to bed by his asthma. He told his friend Ricardo Rojo, when Rojo visited him in Havana, that he had the custom of "really thinking deeply" whenever he was struck by an asthma attack, and that on such occasions he often thought of carrying the revolution to his native Argentina. For this reason, he kept a map of Argentina in the private passage through which he daily entered and left his office. This appears to correlate with certain psychiatric evidence which suggests that most chronic asthmatics tend to be dreamers. At any rate, Che was a dreamer, for only a dreamer could have believed, as he did, that the revolutionary liberation of Latin America was an objective capable of realization in the 1960's.

As for the assertion that Che was an adventurer, this he admitted himself in the following letter, which he wrote to his parents in the spring of 1965 (shortly before he departed from Cuba on a secret mission to help the rebel forces in the Congo):

Dear Parents:

Once again I feel below my heels the ribs of Rosinante. I return to the road with my shield on my arm.

Almost ten years ago, I wrote you another farewell letter. As I remember, I lamented not being a better soldier and a better doctor. The second doesn't interest me any longer. As a soldier I am not so bad.

Nothing in essence has changed, except that I am much more conscious, and my Marxism has taken root and become pure. I believe in the armed struggle as the only solution for those peoples who fight to free themselves, and I am consistent with my beliefs. Many will call me an adventurer, and that I am; only one of a different kind—one of those who risks his skin to prove his beliefs.

It could be that this may be the end. Not that I look for it, but it is within the logical calculus of probabilities. If it is so, I send you a last embrace. I have loved you very much, only I have not known how to express my love. I am extremely rigid in my actions and I believe that at times you did not understand me. It was not easy to understand me. On the other hand, I ask only that you believe in me today.

Now, a will that I have polished with the delight of an artist will sustain my pair of flaccid legs and tired lungs. I will do it!

Remember from time to time this little condottiere [Italian term meaning "soldier of fortune"] of the twentieth century. A kiss to Celia, to Roberto, Juan Martin and Pototin, to Beatriz, to everyone. A large embrace from your recalcitrant prodigal son.

Ernesto

Che knew that his life might well come to a tragic end. In addition to his reference to this in his farewell letter to his parents in the spring of 1965, he also acknowledged the possibility in a letter which he sent at about the same time to his old friend and traveling partner Alberto Granados. In this letter he prophetically wrote: "My rolling house has two legs once again and my dreams will have no frontier—at least until the bullets speak."

In sum, Che was not an insane fanatic, and he did not have a pathological love of bloodshed and human cruelty. However, he was not a normal and contented man. If he had been, he would never have become a revolutionary. He was a dreamer, an adventurer, and a rebel against the established order of things. He was a man deeply incensed by the social injustices which he saw all around him, and motivated by a sincere desire to rectify them. He was the perfect revolutionary—the super-idealist who insists on bringing heaven immediately to earth. Moreover, his willingness to die for his ideals indicates that he possessed far more courage and conviction than the ordinary man. Indeed, the fact that he fought and died for what he believed in makes him stand out in sharp contrast to the vast majority of Latin America's present political leaders, whose opportunism and lack of conviction have left the masses with little hope that their condition will ever be improved by the existing political order.

CHAPTER 2

Che's Theories on Revolutionary Warfare

In the future, any book written on the history of Latin American social and political thought in the twentieth century will surely include a discussion of Che Guevara's ideas about revolution and guerrilla warfare. Today, his writings on this subject are considered required reading for all those interested in understanding the nature of guerrilla warfare and the conditions which recommend its use. Che's book *La Guerra de Guerrillas* (*Guerrilla Warfare*), first published in 1960, is now considered one of the most important works on guerrilla warfare ever written. This book, along with certain articles written by Che, in particular his "Guerra de Guerrillas: un Metodo" ("Guerrilla Warfare: A Method") put forward a complete theory of revolutionary guerrilla warfare, largely based upon the Cuban experience. It is this theory which has provided the guidelines for revolutionary insurrections throughout Latin America in recent years, and which continues to inspire radical groups to go off into the hills and follow the example set by Fidel and Che.

During his days as a guerrilla leader in the Sierra Maestra, Che made it a daily habit to write down his observations in a personal campaign diary. At the end of a long day's march or after an engagement with the enemy, he always sat down somewhere apart from the others to write about the events of the day. On the basis of these notes he was later able to formulate his theories about guerrilla warfare and to write an excellent historical account of the Cuban revolutionary war, entitled *Pasajes de la Guerra Revolucionaria* (*Passages from the Revolutionary War*).

It was Che's belief that the Cuban Revolution clearly demonstrated that the people of Latin America can liberate themselves from dictatorial rule if they resort to guerrilla warfare. In his book *La Guerra de Guerrillas*, Che wrote that the Cuban Revolution had made three fundamental contributions to revolutionary thought in Latin America. First of all, the Cuban experience proved that popular forces could win a war against a professional army. Secondly, it proved that it is not necessary to wait until all the conditions for revolution are present. According to Che, the insurrectional guerrilla *foco* (a Spanish word used to refer to the center of guerrilla operations) can itself create the necessary conditions. Finally, Cuba demonstrated that in Latin America, which is largely underdeveloped, any revolutionary struggle must concentrate on the rural areas and not the cities if it is to succeed. Che claimed that the first two of these contributions in particular refute the arguments of those who claim to be revolutionaries but refuse to take revolutionary action because of the pretext that nothing can be done against a professional army or until all the necessary conditions for revolution exist.

According to Che, a nucleus of from thirty to fifty determined men can establish and consolidate a revolutionary guerrilla *foco* in any country of Latin America, providing they have the cooperation of the people and a perfect knowledge of the terrain upon which they will be operating. Che stressed that the people must believe it is impossible for them to obtain social and economic reforms through peaceful means before they will be inclined to support an insurrectionary guerrilla *foco*. Moreover, he argued that where a government has risen to power by some form of popular consultation, including fraudulent elections, and maintains at least the appearance of constitutional legality, it is impossible to establish and consolidate a guerrilla *foco* because many of the people will still believe that there is some possibility of improving their social and economic condition through legal means.

Che was very critical of those who argue that the revolutionary struggle in Latin America depends upon the mobilization of the discontented urban masses in the cities. He felt that it is far more difficult to carry out a successful insurrection in the cities, where the forces of the existing regimes can be effectively concentrated and utilized, than in the rural areas, where regular troops are at the mercy of a highly mobile guerrilla force supported by the rural population. The support of the rural population, according to Che, is the *sine qua non* of guerrilla warfare. In fact, he defines guerrilla war as a war of the people, led by a fighting vanguard (the nuclear guerrilla force) against the forces of the ruling oligarchies and their foreign backers. Thus, the guerrilla force does not seize power by itself; rather, it serves as a catalyst which inspires the masses themselves to take up arms and overthrow the established regime.

In *La Guerra de Guerrillas*, Che wrote that without the support of the people, a guerrilla force is nothing more than a roving gang of bandits. He noted that both have the same characteristics: homogeneous membership, respect for their leaders, courage, knowledge of the terrain, and appreciation of the correct tactics to employ against numerically superior forces. However, they differ in one fundamental respect: one has the support of the people and the other does not. Consequently, bandits are inevitably hunted down and eliminated, whereas guerrilla forces, which count upon the support of the people, can defeat a professional army and bring about the downfall of the most oppressive regime.

The guerrilla force, according to Che, wins the support of the masses in the rural areas largely by championing their grievances. This means that the guerrillas must present themselves as crusaders intent upon righting the injustices of the prevailing social order. Che believed that the major grievances shared by the rural masses throughout Latin America arise from the almost feudal system of land ownership, whereby the great majority of the peasantry do not own the land upon which they live. Consequently, he saw land reform as the key issue to be used by guerrilla forces in their effort to win the support of the rural masses. In other words, Che argued that the guerrilla must be an agrarian revolutionary who uses the peasantry's hunger for land as the basis for mobilizing their support.

Che also believed that any revolutionary guerrilla force must be the conscience of the people, and that the moral behavior of each guerrilla must be such that the people regard him as a true priest of the social reforms that he advocates. According to Che, the guerrilla must always exercise rigid self-control and never permit himself a single excess or weakness. This means that the guerrilla must be an ascetic whose moral behavior earns him the respect and admiration of the local population. In addition, Che wrote that it is the duty of guerrillas to give technical, economic, and social assistance to the peasantry. In this way, they develop a close relationship with the peasantry, which allows them to win their trust and confidence. Once this relationship has been achieved, it then becomes the task of the guerrillas to indoctrinate the peasantry concerning the fundamental importance of the armed struggle to their liberation from their present state of exploitation and oppression. The successful execution of this task brings into existence a true people's war and the inevitable destruction of the existing regime.

One of Che's most original contributions to the literature on guerrilla warfare is his discussion of the qualities of the guerrilla fighter. According to him, the ideal guerrilla soldier is an inhabitant of the zone in which the nuclear guerrilla *foco* is established. This is because the two most important prerequisites of successful guerrilla warfare are a thorough knowledge of the terrain and the cooperation of the local population. The guerrilla who is an inhabitant of the region in which he is operating knows the terrain and has friends in the area to whom he can turn for help. It follows, therefore, that in Latin America the local *campesino* (peasant) makes the best guerrilla soldier, although Che emphasized that a guerrilla force should not be composed exclusively of *campesinos*.

Che seems to have been describing himself without knowing it when he listed the personal qualities that the ideal guerrilla soldier should have. He stressed audacity and a readiness to take an optimistic attitude at times when an analysis of existing conditions does not warrant it. He also indicated that the guerrilla fighter must be ready to risk his life on an almost daily basis and to voluntarily give it up if the circumstances require it. This of course demands a high degree of devotion to the cause for which the guerrillas are fighting, and, according to Che, such devotion can be sustained only if the guerrilla movement is based upon an ideal or ideals which are meaningful to each guerrilla fighter. He concluded that among nearly all *campesinos* such an ideal is the right to have a piece of land as their own, while the ideal of adequate wages and better social conditions plays a comparable role among guerrillas from the urban working classes, and more abstract ideals, such as freedom, motivate students and intellectuals.

In addition to the moral and psychological qualities that make a good guerrilla fighter, Che stressed that he must also have certain important physical qualities and be able to adapt to the most difficult environmental conditions. As Che himself well knew, the conditions of guerrilla life require the endurance of severe privations, including the lack of food, water, proper clothing, shelter, and medical attention. Moreover, the guerrilla must be able to adapt to a life of almost constant movement in which he is required to march long distances and traverse areas where no ordinary man would ever venture.

Che wrote that in terms of the general pattern of the guerrilla's day-to-day life, combat is the most interesting event that befalls him. Combat, therefore, is both the climax and the greatest joy of the guerrilla's life, and only through combat does he fulfill the purpose for which he exists. Che emphasized that the guerrilla must perform his role as a combatant without any reluctance or weakness, since he must give the enemy no quarter and expect none in return. On the other hand, Che also made the point that wounded and captured enemy soldiers must be treated benevolently by the guerrilla soldier, unless they have committed criminal acts which require that they be tried and executed.

The final objective of a revolutionary guerrilla war, according to Che, is the defeat of the enemy's army and the seizure of political power in the name of the people. However, he made it quite clear that guerrilla warfare cannot in itself bring about victory. He emphasized that it is important to remember that guerrilla warfare is only the first phase of a war of national liberation, and that, unless it develops into a conventional war, the enemy cannot be completely defeated.

Che wrote that in the earliest stages the primary strategy of a revolutionary guerrilla force is to assure its own survival. This means that it must flee from and avoid the enemy forces sent to destroy it. During this phase, it must restrict its offensive activities to lightning attacks on unsuspecting enemy posts or units, and in each case retreat to a secure hiding place before the enemy has a chance to react with its superior forces and weapons. If the guerrilla force succeeds in eluding the enemy forces sent to destroy it, Che assumed, it will increasingly attract recruits from the rural population and gradually enlarge the scale of its operations, striking more frequently at the enemy troops in the zone surrounding the guerrilla *foco*. In this way, the guerrillas begin to weaken and demoralize the enemy's forces. By systematically harassing the enemy through surprise attacks, they also disrupt his communications and force him onto the defensive.

The next phase involves extending the territory of guerrilla activity by sending small groups deep into enemy territory to sabotage and terrorize the enemy's key centers of supply and communications. Meanwhile, the original base of guerrilla operations must be continually strengthened and measures must be taken to indoctrinate the inhabitants of the guerrilla zone. Later, when more men and arms have been obtained and the circumstances appear to warrant an expansion of the conflict, new guerrilla columns are formed and sent to operate in areas behind the enemy's lines.

The final phase of the struggle begins, according to Che, when the guerrilla columns unite and engage the enemy's forces in a conventional war of fixed fronts. It is at this moment that the "people's army" comes into existence, and the drive towards the cities begins. The death knell of the old order comes as the urban masses turn upon the defending troops and the last strongholds of enemy resistance surrender to the people's army. This clears the way for the revolutionary leaders to seize power and begin the building of a new society.

Che warned that a people's army does not emerge spontaneously, and that victory is obtained only after a long and difficult struggle in which the people's forces and their leaders are exposed to repeated attacks by superior forces intent upon annihilating them. He also pointed out that the guerrillas must expect to suffer greatly at the hands of the enemy. Che made this point most effectively in the following passage from his article "Guerrilla Warfare: A Method":

> They [the guerrillas] will perhaps be punished heavily by the enemy's armies. At times they will be separated from each other and those taken prisoner will be martyred. They will be pursued like hunted animals in the areas where they have chosen to operate, with the constant anxiety of having the enemy at their heels and the constant fear that the terrorized peasants will give them away to the repressive troops in order to save their own skins. They will have no other alternative but death or victory, in moments in which death is a thousand times present and victory is a myth about which only a revolutionary can dream.

However, Che argued that even if only a fragment of the original guerrilla nucleus survives, it can continue to spark the revolutionary spirit of the masses and can organize anew to carry on the struggle.

Che believed that war responds to a series of scientific laws, and that those who disregard these laws are destined to be defeated. Since guerrilla warfare is merely one type of war, he claimed that it was governed by the same laws. However, because of its special aspects, Che argued that guerrilla warfare is also governed by a series of accessory laws or principles which must be recognized by any guerrilla force which hopes to succeed.

Since one of the precepts of guerrilla warfare is the enemy's vast superiority in troops as well as in equipment, Che stressed that the guerrillas must utilize special tactics which will allow them to offset the enemy's superiority. These tactics are based upon two essential preconditions: (1) the guerrillas must be highly mobile, and (2) they must possess a much greater knowledge of the terrain over which they will be operating than the enemy. Unless these two preconditions are met, the guerrillas will not have the minimum capabilities required for effectively utilizing the special tactics of guerrilla warfare.

Extreme mobility and a detailed knowledge of the terrain of operations make it possible, in Che's opinion, for the guerrillas to outmaneuver and surprise the numerically superior and better-equipped forces sent against them. With these capabilities, they can strike the enemy when he is off-guard, and then quickly disappear before he can retaliate, thus inflicting heavy casualties on the enemy with very few or no losses of their own.

"Strike and run, wait, watch carefully, and then again strike and run." This, in Che's words, is the primary tactic of guerrilla warfare, to be repeated over and over again until the enemy is demoralized and forced to take a static and essentially defensive posture. The basic characteristics of this tactic are the element of surprise and the rapidity of the guerrillas' attacking and withdrawal maneuvers. The speed and surprise inherent in this tactic give the guerrillas a great advantage over the enemy's larger and better-equipped forces. Moreover, Che noted that it is particularly effective when used at night, and that, for this reason, one of the basic features of guerrilla warfare is night fighting.

Somewhat more static than the hit-and-run technique, but just as effective, is the ambush. This tactic is, of course, as old as war itself and has always been used by the weak against the strong. It requires that the enemy be on the move, ideally, marching in file through a ravine, canyon, or pass, where he can be caught in a devastating crossfire. However, Che made an original contribution to this age-old tactic. In his writings, Che mentions the psychological damage that can be inflicted upon the enemy if the guerrillas follow the practice of always concentrating their fire upon the advance elements of the army units they catch in their ambushes. This confronts the enemy's soldiers with the realization that they can expect almost certain death if they are in the advance positions of a column. This tactic, Che claimed, creates panic among the soldiers and may even lead them to mutiny if they are ordered to take the lead positions in a column marching through a suspected guerrilla area.

In addition to the ambush and the rapid hit-and-run type of attack, Che also wrote about what is called the "minuet tactic." The kind of movement used with this tactic is somewhat analogous to the dance of the same name, and involves surrounding an enemy column with several small groups of men. These groups alternately engage the enemy from different points. As soon as one group retreats, another one initiates an attack from a different direction. As a result, the enemy column is constantly kept off-balance and demoralized. In fact, if the guerrillas have enough men and ammunition, and there is no possibility of the surrounded enemy column receiving outside aid, the guerrillas can annihilate the entire column through the use of this tactic.

Che emphasized that a guerrilla force must never allow itself to be encircled, for experience had shown, he said, that the only really effective way of stamping out a guerrilla force is to encircle the guerrillas in a given area, concentrate as many troops in the circle as possible, and progressively close in around the guerrillas until they are completely liquidated. For this reason, guerrilla warfare is a war without any fixed front or battle lines. According to Che, the guerrillas must appear and disappear at the enemy's rear, at his flanks, and in his midst. In the initial stages, they rarely attempt to hold a given position, since their concern is to avoid encirclement or a frontal encounter with the enemy's superior forces. Instead, their aim is to inflict as many casualties on the enemy's forces as possible without jeopardizing themselves. Confronted with this type of irregular warfare, Che claimed that the enemy's regular army is rendered powerless. Since they are equipped and trained to fight a conventional war or control the street demonstrations of students and workers, they become frightened and completely demoralized when forced to combat the tactics of the guerrillas.

Since one of the most important aspects of guerrilla warfare is the relationship that exists between the guerrillas and the local population, Che believed that the guerrillas should conduct themselves at all times in the most respectful manner towards the civilian population. For this reason, Che advocated they always pay for any goods taken, or at least give a certificate of debt to be paid at some future date. He also emphasized that the zone of guerrilla operations must never be impoverished by the direct action of the guerrillas, and that the local inhabitants must be permitted to sell their products outside the guerrilla zone, except under extreme circumstances. As the guerrilla effort progresses and the whole area of a country comes under their control, then, according to Che, the guerrillas must assume responsibility for governing the civilian population and regulating economic activity in the areas under their control.

Although Che felt sabotage was one of the most effective tactics available to a revolutionary guerrilla movement, he was opposed to terrorism. He believed that terrorism is a negative weapon which can turn the people against a revolutionary movement. Moreover, in his opinion, the results of terrorist attacks are not worth the cost in lives that they entail. On the other hand, he distinguished sabotage (the destruction of essential industries and public works) from terrorism (the systematic use of violence to coerce the population), and advocated the destruction of nearly everything necessary for normal, modern life, e.g., telephone lines, electrical power stations, water mains, sewers, gas pipelines, railroads, radio stations, etc. Yet even in the case of sabotage, Che pointed out that a guerrilla force must consider the social consequences of each act of destruction so as not to cause unnecessary suffering among the urban and rural masses.

For Che, one of the most important characteristics of guerrilla warfare is the difference between the information possessed by the guerrillas and that possessed by the enemy. He saw the situation as one in which the enemy's regular forces must constantly operate in areas where they encounter the sullen silence of the local inhabitants, while the guerrillas can count upon a friend in every house who will pass information about the enemy's movements along to the guerrilla headquarters or the guerrilla force operating in the area. Che believed that this is one of the greatest advantages enjoyed by the guerrillas, and that it should be utilized to the fullest extent.

However, in Che's opinion, a guerrilla force should never confide too much in the local peasantry, since peasants have a natural tendency to talk to their friends and relatives about everything they see and hear. Moreover, in view of the brutal way in which the regular troops treat the local population in an area where guerrillas are know to be operating, he warned that it is to be expected that certain members of the population will give the enemy information about the guerrillas in order to escape torture or mistreatment.

Since Che conceived of guerrilla warfare as a revolutionary war of the people in which the guerrillas serve as the revolutionary vanguard, he repeatedly emphasized throughout his writings that the support of the masses was crucial to the success of any guerrilla insurgency. Therefore, he was preoccupied with treating in detail how a guerrilla force secures and develops popular support. For this reason, his writings on revolutionary guerrilla war come closer to being a manual on how to organize and successfully execute a popular revolution than a theoretical work on military strategy and tactics *per se*.

As perceptive and eloquent as Che's writings on guerrilla warfare are, they do not provide a valid blueprint for replicating the Cuban Revolution elsewhere in Latin America. In the first place,

Che's basic premise is questionable, i.e., that the Cuban experience provides a model which revolutionary movements throughout Latin American will find it useful, if not necessary, to follow. To make generalizations based upon one case is always inadvisable, but to do so with a view toward providing others with a formula for fomenting revolution elsewhere is an extremely dangerous undertaking.

Most revolutionary movements in Latin America over the last five years have been based on Che's contention that a small band of from thirty to fifty guerrillas can create the conditions required for a revolutionary victory in any country of Latin America. To date, every one of these movements, including the one directed by Che himself, has failed to demonstrate that an insurrectionary guerrilla *foco* located in the rural areas can provide the foundation for a successful revolution. One of the reasons for this is that, even in the Cuban case, the revolution was the culmination of more than either Che or many others have perceived.

It has been said, with some justification, that the Cubans have not understood their own revolution. Blinded by the myths and legends that now surround their revolution, the Cubans believe that theirs was a peasant revolution, mounted by a small guerrilla force which came down out of the mountains and liberated the cities. There is much more to the story of the Cuban Revolution than this. To be sure, the guerrillas were the symbol of the revolution, and they played a crucial role in its development. However, Cuba's urban middle classes, who threw their weight behind the guerrillas because of their hatred of Batista, and the weakness of the Cuban army, which was unhappy about defending an unpopular regime, may well have been the decisive factors. Moreover, if Castro had put forward a more radical program prior to his seizure of power, the revolutionary movement against Batista would *not* have been able to acquire the magnitude which made possible its victory. Castro cleverly presented himself as a moderate leader, promising elections and a constitutional government once Batista's dictatorial regime was toppled.

Actually, the Cuban experience may well have made another

Cuban-type revolution in Latin America impossible. It is hard to imagine a guerrilla movement today either (1) deceiving the middle classes into believing it has moderate political aims or (2) winning the support of U.S. and international public opinion as romantic freedom-fighters combating a tyrannical regime. The ruling elites in Latin America have learned a lot from the Cuban revolution. They now know that a revolutionary guerrilla force must be eliminated as soon as it appears, that the army must be effectively trained in counterinsurgency warfare, and that serious efforts must be made to win the support of the peasantry or at least to forestall their giving support to a revolutionary movement.

However, the real discrepancy in Che's theories appears to be his emphasis upon the rural population as the popular base for any successful revolutionary movement in Latin America. First of all, the armies of a number of Latin American countries, through the use of modern counterinsurgency tactics learned by their officers at the U.S. Army's special training school in the Canal Zone, have shown that they can defeat Cuban-type guerrilla movements operating among their rural populations. But even more important is the obvious fact, recognized by an increasing number of Latin American revolutionaries themselves, that the main breeding grounds for revolution in Latin America are the cities. The cities are being literally inundated with migrants from the rural areas. Hoping to break away from the poverty and misery of rural Latin America, they find waiting for them in the cities unemployment and worse living conditions than they had in the rural areas. The frustration and discontent which derive from this situation provide a natural basis for revolution. Thus, today and in the future, it is not the rural areas but the exploding urban centers that offer the most appropriate base for revolutionary movements in Latin America.

CHAPTER 3

Why Che Left Cuba

Any analysis of why Che Guevara died in Bolivia must take into account the reasons he left Cuba in 1965, for it was the motives behind his departure from Cuba that eventually led him to Bolivia.

There has been a great deal of speculation over why Che resigned his cabinet post in Fidel Castro's government and disappeared from public view in 1965. At the time of Che's disappearance, many believed that Che and Castro had come to a serious disagreement and that Che had been either imprisoned or secretly executed. There were also reports that Che had been killed in the Dominican Republic during the civil war that took place there in the spring of 1965. Later on, there was again speculation that Castro or elements within the Cuban regime had eliminated Che because of his opposition to certain policies advocated by the pro-Soviet wing of the Cuban Communist Party. However, it is now clear that none of these speculations were correct.

By the beginning of 1964, it appears to have been evident even to Che that his four-year plan initiated in 1961 to industrialize Cuba was a failure. He had underestimated the difficulties in-

volved in transforming Cuba from an agrarian economy domi-
nated by the production and exportation of sugar to an industrialized economy characterized by diversification and the extensive
application of modern technology. He seems to have trusted
blindly in his program of accelerated industrialization, to the
extent that he even predicted his four-year plan would double the
standard of living in Cuba by 1965. Actually, his industrialization
program succeeded only in disorganizing the agricultural sector by
diverting manpower to the urban areas. Agricultural production in
Cuba during 1961, 1962, and 1963 fell below the levels attained
prior to the revolution.

On the basis of what Che told friends such as Ricardo Rojo
and others, it is possible to ascertain what his thinking was during
this period. In the first place, it is clear that Che was forced to
admit that Cuba would have to return to its historical mode of
livelihood, i.e., the production of sugar for export. Yet he was not
willing to accept the recommendations of his Soviet advisors that
Cuba abandon the goal of becoming an industrialized country. He
felt strongly that Cuba's economic relations with the socialist bloc
of nations should not be the same as those between capitalist
countries. If Cuba could not industrialize by itself as a result of
the underdeveloped character of its economy, then Che argued
that the more developed socialist countries had an obligation to
help Cuba. He thought the Soviet Union should finance Cuba's
long-term efforts to industrialize, instead of expecting her to remain the socialist bloc's sugar mill.

Che found little sympathy for his ideas among the Russians.
They regarded his plans to industrialize Cuba as totally impractical. Even if Cuba were to succeed in transforming its economy
with Soviet assistance, they argued that there would be an insuffi-
cient market for Cuba's manufactured goods. They pointed out
that Cuba's internal market was not large enough to make the production of its own manufactured items economically justifiable,
and that in view of Cuba's political isolation it could not expect to
export its products to any of its neighbors. When Che countered
that Cuba would have an export market in Latin America as soon

as the revolution was carried to other countries of Central and South America, the Russians made it quite clear that they were not willing to risk basing their support on this eventuality.

Moscow's opposition to his plans led Che to conclude that the Russians presented almost as much of an obstacle to the forces of revolutionary change as the United States. He became convinced, moreover, that Moscow and Washington had entered into a tacit agreement to respect each other's spheres of influence, and that, as part of this agreement, Moscow had promised to restrain Havana from promoting revolution in Latin America. Che decided that Cuba had no other alternative than to reduce its dependence upon the Soviet Union so that it could pursue its own domestic and foreign policies without outside interference. He became convinced that Cuba should firmly align itself with the neutral nations of Africa and Asia. In this way, he thought, Cuba could play an important role in international affairs and promote socialism independently of Moscow. This idea motivated him to travel extensively throughout Africa and Asia during late 1964 and early 1965.

Che's appearance in Algeria during February, 1965, as a "Cuban observer" at the second conference of the Organization of Afro-Asian Solidarity took the form of a personal crusade to create an anti-imperialist front among the neutral nations of the third world. He severely admonished the Soviet Union for evading its responsibility to support popular revolutions in the third world, and for pursuing a selfish foreign policy which ignored the international objectives of the working class. In March, he made a secret trip to Red China in order to discuss with Mao Tse-tung the possibility of obtaining Chinese backing for his plan to create revolutionary guerrilla movements in various parts of the world. Mao, however, made it clear he was more interested in seeing Che stay in Cuba for the purpose of defending the Chinese position against Soviet "revisionism."

When Che returned to Cuba in March, 1965, he had already begun to consider resigning his position in the Cuban government in order to devote all his efforts to furthering the armed struggle against imperialism. Since he had played such an important role in the Cuban revolution without being Cuban, he assumed he would be able to do the same elsewhere, not only in Latin America, but in Africa and Asia as well.

Shortly after Che returned to Havana, he met with Fidel Castro to discuss the results of his travels and his recommendations regarding Cuba's position in international affairs. At this meeting, Castro was forced to reject Che's suggestion that Cuba should follow a foreign policy independent of Moscow. Castro could not accept Che's proposals since he was under both external and internal pressures to move Cuba closer to Moscow. In fact, the old-guard Communists within Castro's regime, led by Anibal Escalante, were pressing Castro to come out openly in favor of Moscow's position in the Sino-Soviet conflict. Their arguments were greatly strengthened by Cuba's dependence upon Soviet aid. According to Escalante's group, Cuba was dependent upon Moscow for both its economic survival and military protection against an American invasion. Cuba should, therefore, act in accordance with reality and openly express its solidarity with the Soviet Union. For the reasons stated earlier, Che could not accept this position.

Che realized that Castro had no other alternative but to give in to Escalante and the Soviets. Che understood that his continued presence in the government, in light of his policy disagreements with the Soviets and with Castro himself, would greatly prejudice the Cuban leader's position. He also realized that it would be impossible for him to remain in Cuba divested of his former high posts. In view of the circumstances, Che decided to resign from the government and leave Cuba. Since Castro was under increasing pressure from the old guard of the Cuban Communist Party to remove Che, he did not try to talk Che out of resigning when the latter indicated that he thought it was time for him to go elsewhere and further the revolution against imperialism.

Che's disagreement with Castro regarding Cuba's relationship with Moscow did not end the longstanding friendship between them. Nor did it lead Castro to abandon his desire to see Cuba play an important role in the international struggle against imperialism. Shortly after Che told Castro that he intended to leave Cuba, Castro supported Che's plan to take a contingent of Cubans to assist the left-wing rebels in the Congo, who were fighting against the pro-Western regime of Moise Tshombe.

Before his return to Havana, Che had met Gaston Soumialet, one of the Congolese rebel leaders, in Cairo, and they had discussed his ideas about revolution, guerrilla warfare, and imperialism. Apparently, it was during this meeting that Soumialet invited Che to come to the Congo and help train the Congolese rebel forces. It was not until after his return to Cuba, however, that Che decided that the most appropriate place to put his guerrilla experience into practice would be the Congo. The Congo appealed to him largely because of his fascination with the idea of linking the nations of Africa, Asia, and Latin America together into a powerful anti-imperialist force.

In order to prepare for his mission to the Congo, Che removed himself from public view at the end of March, 1965. But by the end of April, his disappearance had begun to cause a great deal of speculation both inside and outside Cuba. On April 30, Castro was interviewed by a number of reporters, and in response to their questions about Che, he answered that he could say only that Che would always be where he could be of most use to the revolution. This statement, however, only served to intensify the speculation and rumors regarding Che's disappearance. As a result, Che wrote a personal letter of resignation, which he hoped would squash the speculations about his disappearance. This letter, which Castro did not make public until October, 1965, also appears to have been designed to absolve Castro and the Cuban government of all responsibility for the actions Che was undertaking in the Congo:

Fidel:

I remember at this hour many things, when we met at Maria Antonia's house, when you suggested that I come to Cuba, and the tension of the last minute preparations. One day they came around asking who to advise in case of death, and its real possibility struck us all. Afterward, we knew that it was certain, that in a revolution you die or triumph (if the revolution is a true one). Many of our comrades were left behind on the long road to victory. Today everything has a less dramatic tone because we are all more mature, but the same thing is repeating itself. I feel I have completed that part of my duty that has tied me to the Cuban revolution and so I say goodbye to you, our comrades, and to your people, who are now mine too.

I formally renounce my post in the directorate of the party, my post as minister, my rank of commandant, and my status as a Cuban. There is nothing legal that ties me to Cuba, only ties of another type that cannot be broken as in the case of offices. Making a summary of my past life, I think that I have worked with sufficient honesty and dedication to consolidate the success of the revolution. My only fault of any gravity is that I did not confide in you at the beginning in the Sierra Maestra and have not understood with sufficient clarity your qualities as a leader and revolutionary.

I have lived magnificent days at your side and I have felt the pride of belonging to our people in the dark and bright days of the Caribbean crisis. Rarely has a statesman shone as brightly as in those days. I feel proud of having followed you without hesitation, identifying myself with your way of thinking, seeing and appreciating both the dangers and principles. Other lands of the world now claim the assistance of my modest efforts. I can do what you now are prevented from doing because of your responsibility at the helm of Cuba, and so the time has come to separate. Let it be known that I do this both in pleasure and sorrow: here I leave the purest of my hopes as a builder and the most cherished of my loved ones and I leave a people who admitted me as one of their sons; this lacerates part of my spirit. To new fields of battle I will take the faith that you have given me, the revolutionary spirit of my people, and the feeling of carrying out the most sacred of duties: to fight against imperialism wherever it exists; this comforts and cures my pain abundantly.

Once again I say that I free Cuba of all responsibility, except that which comes from her example. If my last hour should come under other skies, my last thought will be for the Cuban people and especially for you. I am grateful for your teaching and example, and I will be faithful to you until my last act. I have always identified myself with the foreign policies of our revolution and will continue to do so. Wherever I go I will feel the responsibility of being a Cuban revolutionary, and I will act as one. I leave nothing material to my wife and children; and this doesn't bother me for I am happy that it is this way. I ask nothing for them, since the state will provide them enough to live and will educate them. There are many things I could tell you and our people, but I feel that this is not necessary. Words cannot express what I want to say, and it is not worth while to fill sheets of paper. Victory always! Country or death! My embrace with all revolutionary fervor.

Che

Che left for the Congo sometime during July, 1965, leading a hand-picked group of Cubans who had fought with him and Castro in the Sierra Maestra. Their departure was carefully planned by Cuban intelligence, which even managed to plant a false report in the Dominican Republic that indicated that Che had arrived in Santo Domingo in April and had been killed shortly thereafter in one of the street battles that took place there during the civil war. Thus, while the CIA was looking for evidence of Che's presence in the Dominican Republic, he and his companions were able to leave Cuba for the Congo under the cover of complete secrecy.

In the Congo, Che and the Cubans with him served as instructors and advisers to the rebel troops under the leadership of Gaston Soumialet and Pierre Mulele. Their task was not an easy one, for they had to train illiterate tribesmen to fight against President Tshombe's well-equipped European mercenaries.

It is difficult to say whether Castro supported Che's mission to the Congo primarily because he wanted to satisfy the desires of his close friend or because he was unwilling to give up completely, for the sake of the Russians, an adventurous foreign policy. At any rate, he was soon forced to ask Che and his group to leave the Congo. In February, 1966, Castro publicly denounced what he described as a Chinese plot to subvert the Cuban army. Among other things, he accused the Chinese of having distributed anti-Soviet literature to Cuban troops. In retaliation, the Chinese withdrew their advisers and withheld a shipment of rice which they had promised Cuba. This break between Peking and Havana had an almost immediate effect on Che's presence in the Congo. The Chinese, who were the principal financial backers of the Congolese rebel movement, pressured Soumialet and Mulele to force Che and his Cuban contingent to leave the Congo. At the same time, Moscow strongly urged Castro to order Che and his group out of the Congo, fearing that the discovery of his presence there might create a serious international crisis.

When he received word from Cuba to return immediately, Che refused to leave. Castro then sent two personal envoys, majors Aragones and Drake, to convince Che that it was absolutely necessary for him and his companions to leave the Congo without delay. They informed Che that his presence in the Congo had placed Cuba in a very compromising position, and that Castro wanted him to return to Havana with his companions before their presence there was discovered. Thus, in March, 1966 (approximately a year after Che had disappeared from public view), Che left the Congo as secretly as he had entered. It was a bitter blow to Che to return to Cuba after spending nine months in the Congo without having anything to show for his efforts. The experience, however, seems to have made Che even more determined than ever to undertake a successful revolutionary mission outside of Cuba.

Che's return to Cuba was never made public. He remained in hiding during the entire period that he stayed there. Almost immediately after his return, he began to plan a new mission which would not have the limitations of his abortive undertaking in the Congo. He chose Bolivia as the site for a revolutionary guerrilla *foco*, which he planned to organize and lead himself. In October, 1966, he left Cuba, as secretly as he had entered, to begin this undertaking.

CHAPTER 4

Why Che Chose Bolivia

ⅬⅬⅬⅬⅬⅬⅬⅬⅬⅬⅬⅬⅬⅬⅬⅬⅬⅬⅬⅬⅬⅬⅬⅬⅬⅬ

The land where Che met his tragic death is a hauntingly beautiful and almost primeval country of towering mountains, cold, windswept vistas, and deep tropical valleys. It has such an other-worldly atmosphere and such unusual colors and geography that the visitor feels he is on another planet rather than in the heart of the South American continent.

Bolivia is divided into two distinctive parts by the massive wall of the Andes Mountains, which traverses the country from north to south. Bolivia west of the Andes perhaps can best be described as a Latin American Tibet. This part of the country is situated on the *altiplano*, the great high plateau of South America. Here the descendents of the Incas, with their herds of llamas, live a bleak existence some two-and-a-half miles above sea level. The vastness and barrenness of this windy plateau give it a beauty all its own, and anyone who has been to this part of the world carries with him unforgettable memories of magnificent panoramas, blue skies filled with clouds that look close enough to touch, and snow-covered peaks bathed in the soft, multicolored light of an indescribably beautiful sunset.

Located on the *altiplano* are Bolivia's major mining centers and the focal point of national politics, the capital city of La Paz. Situated at 11,900 feet in a basin on the *altiplano*, La Paz is the highest capital city in the world. The only approach to the city is from the *altiplano*. Consequently, the first view one receives of La Paz is from some 2,000 feet directly above it. The view takes one's breath away. Far below sprawls the glittering city and, in the distance beyond, the snowy peaks of Mount Illimani tower to a height of over 21,000 feet.

La Paz is a fascinating blend of the old and new. Together with modern buildings and late-model American cars, one sees churches built by the Spaniards three centuries ago, and in every street Indian women with their characteristic bowler hats, colorful shawls, and babies carried on their backs. It is a bustling, sunny city, filled with color and an atmosphere of excitement.

Over the mountains from La Paz lies the city of Cochabamba, an important agricultural center in the heart of a 8,400-foot-high valley where the climate is mildly temperate and the soil quite fertile. Farther east, the mountains drop toward the tropical savannahs and plains of eastern Bolivia. The most important city in this area is Santa Cruz, located at the foot of the eastern slopes of the Andes. Santa Cruz is known for its colonial Spanish architecture and its beautiful women of Spanish descent, but today it has all the characteristics of a boom town. The Bolivian government, with U.S. assistance, has invested heavily in the area and is encouraging Indians from the *altiplano* to come to the various colonization projects located in the surrounding province. The growing economy of the area is based on sugar, cotton, rice, and oil. Approximately two hundred miles south of Santa Cruz lies the town of Camiri, the only other sizable urban community in the eastern part of the country. Camiri is Bolivia's oil center, and although it is not comparable to Santa Cruz in either importance or size, it too is experiencing an economic boom.

Despite the fact that the eastern portion of Bolivia accounts for approximately 70 per cent of the total land area of the country, only about one-fourth of Bolivia's small population of four million lives east of the Andes. This means that the heartland of Bolivia is located on the *altiplano*. It is there that the vast majority of the country's population live and there that the loci of economic and political power are to be found. Most of the important events in Bolivian political history have taken place on the *altiplano*. In 1825, Bolivia formally declared her independence from Spain after some sixteen years of almost uninterrupted warfare. During this time, most of the major battles were fought on the *altiplano*, the focal point being Lake Titicaca, the sacred sea of the Incas and one of the highest lakes in the world. Since independence, the stormy political history of Bolivia has been scarred by more than 150 uprisings, revolts, and coups d'etat. Nearly all of these have centered around the *altiplano* cities of Sucre (the country's first capital), Oruro (Bolivia's main mining center), Cochabamba, and La Paz. The two most important exceptions to this geographic pattern were the war of the Pacific in 1879, in which Bolivia lost her seacoast to Chile, and the Chaco War of 1930–1932, a bloody dispute with Paraguay which resulted in the loss of more than fifty thousand Bolivian troops and a sizable chunk of the Gran Chaco area in the Southeast.

Bolivia's humiliating defeat and territorial loss to Paraguay in the Chaco War led to much internal political turmoil and the demand for major reforms. Returning veterans of the Chaco War organized and provided the fuel for radical political movements among the miners and urban workers that ultimately brought about the revolution of 1952. This event broke the historical pattern of Bolivian politics and destroyed the traditional social order. The *Movimiento Nacionalista Revolucionario* (National Revolutionary Movement) let by Victor Paz Estenssoro, eliminated the professional army with the help of armed workers and miners. Shortly thereafter the new government nationalized the major foreign-owned mining operations in the country and set about diversifying the economy. Of even greater significance, however, was that the government decreed universal suffrage and enacted a national land reform program. As a result, Bolivia's Indian masses gained the dignity of citizenship and were freed from their centuries-old serfdom.

In November, 1964, Paz Estenssoro's MNR government fell victim to the new army which it had established after the 1952 revolution. In classic Latin American style, the military staged a coup d'état and forced Paz Estenssoro to leave the country. His successor was General Rene Barrientos, who had been Bolivia's vice-president and former air force chief of staff. Following the coup, Barrientos appointed a large number of military officers to key posts in the government and doubled the country's defense budget. Under the pretext of correcting the revolutionary excesses of the former regime, he also took a variety of measures designed to stifle all effective political opposition to his regime, particularly the miners and the National Revolutionary Movement. Barrientos, who has been referred to as a Latin American Captain Marvel because of his flamboyant behavior, built a popular base of support around the peasant unions created out of the 1952 revolution. Consequently, in 1966 he felt confident enough to allow a government-controlled election, in which he was formally elected to the presidency of the country. However, his main source of support was the military. Behind Barrientos loomed the very visible figure of General Alfredo Ovando, the commander-in-chief of the Bolivian armed forces at the time and now the head of the present regime.

On his return to Cuba from the Congo, Che found solace in the fact that one of his grandest dreams, an intercontinental organization representing the underdeveloped countries of the world, with its headquarters in Cuba, had been founded only a few months before by Fidel Castro. From January 3 to 15, 1966, the first conference of the Organization of Solidarity of Asian, African, and Latin American Peoples—referred to popularly as the "Tricontinental"—was held in Havana, with some four hundred delegates from the underdeveloped world attending. As it turned out, Che's revolutionary ideas were the central topic of discussion among the delegates, and this undoubtedly reinforced his determination to continue his efforts to extend the Cuban Revolution to other areas. Thus, he immediately began to plan the realization of one of his oldest dreams: the liberation of Latin America's oppressed and exploited masses. This dream was bolstered by his belief that Cuba would become truly independent of Moscow only when additional revolutionary governments were established in Latin America which could provide support to Cuba.

As Fidel states in his introduction to Che's Bolivian diary, Che assigned himself to the mission in Bolivia. However, he would never have gone to Bolivia without Fidel's approval and his promise of support. Why, then, did Fidel support Che's mission to Bolivia? Apparently, by the spring of 1966 Fidel had become quite alarmed over Cuba's faltering prestige due to her failure to make good her promise to carry the armed revolutionary struggle to the rest of Latin America. It seems Fidel decided to support Che's desire to establish a guerrilla movement in Latin America in the belief that if it succeeded it would strengthen Cuba's revolutionary stance in Latin America. Evidently he was also willing to risk incurring the Soviet Union's displeasure and any sanctions which the Russians might bring to bear against Cuba for supporting such an operation.

It appears Che considered several other countries, Peru and Argentina in particular, before choosing Bolivia as the site of his guerrilla operation. There was nothing he would have liked better than to bring the revolution to his native Argentina. This was something he had planned for many years. But it was obvious that the situation in Argentina was not favorable for such an undertaking in 1966 or 1967.

In 1964, a Cuban-inspired guerrilla force attempted to establish itself in northern Argentina, but the effort ended in total failure a few months later without having realized a single military engagement. The leader of this group, an Argentine named Jorge Masetti, had been a close friend of Che's in Cuba, and it is clear that Masetti and Che together planned the Argentine undertaking in early 1963. Their objective at the time was to establish a chain of guerrilla bands from Peru to northern Argentina. However, Masetti's small force was defeated by the harsh environment of northern Argentina and by his inability to attract any popular support. In the end, those members of his guerrilla band who did not die from starvation and exposure were either taken prisoner or killed by the Argentine police. The death of Masetti and the three Cubans from Che's own bodyguard, who had gone with him to help establish the guerrilla movement in Argentina, was a bitter reminder to Che that Argentina was not the most suitable place for him to establish a guerrilla force.

As for Peru, the situation there was no more favorable than that in Argentina. In 1966, that country had an elected civilian regime with a moderately progressive program. Moreover, the government and the army had effectively suppressed several guerrilla uprisings in isolated parts of the country during the preceding two years. Che also considered Colombia, Venezuela, and Brazil, but never very seriously. In the end, Bolivia was chosen because it was considered to have the best revolutionary potential and because it afforded the ideal strategic location. Che had lived in Bolivia for a short time after he finished medical school in 1953. His impression of the country at that time undoubtedly influenced his choice of Bolivia in 1966. As has been previously mentioned, he was there during a period when the country was literally infected with revolutionary enthusiasm. Less than a year before, thousands of miners, *campesinos*, and deserters from the Bolivian army had revolted and brought down the then-existing military regime. When Che arrived in La Paz in 1953, the old army had been destroyed, the largest foreign-owned mines in the country had been nationalized, and the *campesinos* had taken possession of the land under the sanction of the new government's agrarian reform law. The streets were filled with singing and with loud demonstrations, and everywhere he saw the armed *campesinos* and workers of the revolutionary militia. He surely must have thought of these armed *campesinos* and workers in 1966 when he chose Bolivia as the place to initiate his revolutionary movement, firmly believing that the revolution of those days had been subsequently betrayed by opportunistic politicians and generals corrupted by *yanqui* dollars.

A great deal of Che's information on Bolivia appears to have come from two brothers, Coco and Inti Peredo. These young Bolivian Communists had visited Cuba in 1962 and 1965. They had met Che there and discussed with him the possibility of bringing the revolution to Bolivia. They assured him that the country was ripe for a Cuban-type revolution and that all that was needed was Cuban support. The Peredo brothers continued to convey this optimistic picture to Che and the Cuban government after 1965. Thus, when Che in 1966 began searching for a country in Latin America where he could locate a guerrilla movement, he consulted the Peredo brothers. They promptly informed him that there was widespread discontent in Bolivia with the military-backed regime of President Rene Barrientos, and that his government could fall at any moment. They also spoke of the country's strong revolutionary tradition, of the visible and often-resented American presence in the country's economic and political affairs, and of how the mining centers were virtual caldrons of rebellion. Finally, they told Che what he and the Cuban intelligence service already knew, that the Bolivian security and military forces were perhaps the most ineffective and badly organized in Latin America.

The reports of the Peredo brothers were confirmed by other reports distorted by the wishful thinking of young Castroites, or the mercenary calculations of certain Bolivian Communist leaders intent on attracting Cuban funds. As a result, Che decided that his chances in Bolivia were more than satisfactory. He minimized the fact that Bolivia's Communists were badly split along pro-Moscow and pro-Peking lines, and that the pro-Moscow Communist leader in Bolivia had told Fidel during the Tricontinental conference that he was interested in establishing a guerrilla *foco* himself. Che thought that once he arrived on the scene he would be able to unify all the various revolutionary factions in the country behind his guerrilla movement.

Bolivia was also chosen by Che because of its strategic importance, for it lies in the *corazón* ("heart") of South America and borders most of the major countries on the continent (i.e., Argentina, Brazil, Chile, and Peru). From Bolivia, the revolution could then extend in every direction and inflame all of South America.

Having decided on Bolivia, Che selected the southeast of the country for his initial guerrilla *foco*. He chose the southeast because it offered access to neighboring Argentina, Brazil, and Paraguay. In addition, he assumed that in this area, because of its isolation and sparse population, his guerrilla force would be able to develop without being discovered before it was ready to begin operations.

The specific location chosen as the central base of operations was the Ñancahuazú River valley. In this tropical, heavily forested valley, Che planned to train the nucleus of his guerrilla movement, build fortifications, and establish caches of supplies and arms. Once his force was ready for combat, he planned to move north and threaten three of Bolivia's major cities: Cochabamba, Santa Cruz, and Sucre. This would enable the guerrillas to control the railway line that runs from northern Argentina to Santa Cruz, as well as to cut the Gulf Oil Company pipeline that runs from Santa Cruz to Camiri. Later, Che planned to locate a second guerrilla base further east, on the slopes of the Andes. His schedule forecast the beginning of military operations in the spring of 1967, following six months of preparation. In the opening phase, he planned to divide his force into several small bands and have them strike simultaneously at a number of widely dispersed points north of the Ñancahuazú. In this way he hoped to force the Bolivian army to disperse its forces over a large area, while his guerrillas made a slow withdrawal toward the Ñancahuazú, where they could rely upon previously established caches of supplies and the fortifications. If the inexperienced Bolivian army attempted to follow the guerrillas into the Ñancahuazú River valley they would be at their mercy. As his guerrillas demonstrated their capacity to win victories against the Bolivian army, Che reasoned that the *campesinos* and miners would come to the support of the movement.

Che assumed that once the Bolivian guerrilla movement was well established and drawing widespread support and public attention, conditions would become more favorable for guerrilla operations in Peru and Argentina. He planned to have a guerrilla group operating in the Ayacucho region of Peru by the end of 1967 and another force in northern Argentina sometime after that. The Bo-

livian movement was to be a training ground for the nucleus of
both the Peruvian and Argentinian forces.

Che revealed his overall strategy in the message he sent to the
second conference of the Tricontinental in 1967. It is clear that he
believed a successful guerrilla insurgency in Bolivia would force
the United States to commit itself directly to the contest, creating
a second Vietnam in the heart of South America. And, once additional guerrilla movements emerged in Peru and Argentina, he believed the United States would rapidly exhaust itself trying to sup-
press them and the original uprising in Bolivia.

That Che planned to create another Vietnam in Bolivia is clear
from his message to the Tricontinental conference. His conception
of the course of events that would follow the appearance of his
guerrilla movement in Bolivia is revealed in the following passage:

> Little by little the obsolete weapons that are sufficient for the
> suppression of small armed bands will be converted by the
> Americans into modern arms, and American advisers will be
> converted into combatants, until, in a given moment, they will
> see themselves obligated to send increasing quantities of regular
> troops to assure relative stability of a power whose puppet
> national army disintegrates before the attacks of the guerrillas.
> This is the way of Vietnam, it is the way that should be fol-
> lowed by others, and it is the way that *will* be followed in
> Latin America. . . .

Che was counting on American involvement in Bolivia and saw
this as a means of gaining the support of both Bolivian and international public opinion.

As for the ultimate goal of the revolutionary movement Che
was hoping to build in Bolivia, this too was revealed in his message to the Tricontinental conference. He said:

> We can summarize our hopes for victory as follows: the destruc-
> tion of imperialism through the elimination of its strongest
> bulwark: the imperial dominion of the United States of Amer-
> ica. This will be accomplished through the gradual liberation

of its subject peoples, either one by one or by groups, drawing the enemy into a difficult struggle outside of its territory; and cutting it off from its bases of sustenance, i.e., its dependent territories.

Bolivia was to be the first step in a grandiose plan to liberate all of Latin America from U.S. influence and convert it into a bastion of socialism. Everything, therefore, depended upon successfully establishing in Bolivia a guerrilla force that would develop into a revolutionary movement of continental dimensions.

CHAPTER 5

Preparation of the Guerrilla *Foco* in the Southeast of Bolivia

பாபாபாபாபாபாபாபாபாபாபாபாபாபாபாபr

Che could not seek the support of the pro-Peking Communists in Bolivia because of his promise to Fidel that he would not deal with this group. On the other hand, he distrusted the leaders of Bolivia's pro-Moscow Communist Party. Consequently, he relied primarily upon a small number of Castroites within the pro-Moscow group to make the preliminary preparations for his guerrilla operation. These were individuals who had previously spent some time in Cuba and whom Che knew personally. He felt they could be trusted to lay the groundwork for his operation without telling even the leadership of their party what they were doing.

The most important of Che's Bolivian contacts was Coco Peredo. As mentioned earlier, Coco and his brother Inti had helped to convince Che that Bolivia was the ideal base for a guerrilla operation. Because of this and perhaps because Che saw these two brothers as the future Raul and Fidel Castro of Bolivia, he entrusted them with the most important aspects of the preliminary preparations for his guerrilla *foco*.

The Peredo brothers owned and operated a taxi in La Paz. This gave them a perfect cover for their clandestine activities. Sometime during the summer of 1966, they both traveled to the southeast and located themselves in Camiri, Bolivia's petroleum center. There they made friends with some of the local inhabitants and let it be known that they were interested in buying land in the area north of Camiri for the purpose of establishing a ranch and cereal farm.

In September, they succeeded in buying an abandoned ranch in a largely uninhabited region near the Ñancahuazú River, some fifty miles north of Camiri. In addition, they rented some adjacent property from their only neighbor, Ciro Argañaraz, a local landowner and cattle rancher.

While Inti returned to La Paz to take care of their personal affairs, Coco began readying the ranch for the arrival of Che and his Cuban comrades. He contracted two local men to work the ranch and planted several different varieties of cereals. He also bought some cattle, hogs, and poultry. During this period, Coco traveled the winding dirt road from the ranch to Camiri in his new Toyota jeep almost daily. On this road, about twelve miles from the ranch, is the small village of Lagunillas. Coco stopped there on several occasions to buy vegetables and fruits. The large amounts of supplies which he transported to the ranch in his jeep aroused the suspicion of many of the local villagers. Many of them, as well as the landowner, Argañaraz, assumed that the Peredo brothers were either cocaine merchants or cattle thieves.

Meanwhile, in La Paz Che's other Bolivian collaborators made arrangements for receiving Che's group and their equipment. They obtained a house and a warehouse in the center of the city, where they stored arms and ammunition, which they received hidden in bags of cement mix. These were shipped from Cuba to the port of Arica in northern Chile and from there sent by rail to La Paz.

One of Che's prime contacts in La Paz during this period, and later the only female member of his guerrilla force, was a woman known by the code name of Tania. Her real name was Tamara Bunke. She was an Argentine who had spent several years in Cuba. While there, she became a member of the small circle of Argentines who met frequently at Che's house. Tania left Cuba and entered Bolivia in 1964 with a false Argentine passport. In early 1965, she obtained a job working for Gonzalo López, director of information in the presidential palace. In addition to working for López, Tania also successfully passed herself off as a professor of languages. This gave her an opportunity to travel widely throughout the country, ostensibly for the purpose of studying the languages and folk songs of the Indian population. In her spare time she worked her way into some of the capital's artistic, cultural, and diplomatic circles. Her contacts provided Che with valuable information and assistance. Through her direct access to documents and forms in the Information Office of the Presidency she was later able to provide Che and some of his Cuban companions with very impressive credentials that allowed them to travel quite freely within the country.

Everything indicates that Che arrived in Cochabamba, Bolivia's second most important city, around the 1st of November, 1966, on a plane from São Paolo, Brazil. He entered Bolivia as a cleanshaven, bald man wearing glasses. He had two false Uruguayan passports, and it is not clear which of the two he actually used to enter Bolivia. The passports were issued under the names of Ramón Benítez and Adolfo Mena. The fingerprints on both passports are exactly the same as those that have been identified by various governments as belonging to Che. The photographs on both passports are also the same. On close examination they reveal a cleanshaven, bald Che Guevara wearing glasses. Both passports have the same dates of entry and departure from Madrid airport.

Che was accompanied by a Cuban known by the code name of Pacho. Upon arrival they contacted Tania, and she gave Che a truly extraordinary document: it accredited Che (Adolfo Mena, in this case) as a special envoy of the Organization of American States. According to this document, he was in Bolivia for the purpose of conducting research on the social and economic relations prevailing in the rural areas of Bolivia.

(Translation of the document
which Tania gave Che)

CREDENTIAL EXTENDED BY GONZALO LOPEZ, DIRECTOR OF INFORMATION OF THE PRESIDENCY OF THE REPUBLIC, TO ADOLFO MENA, FUNCTIONARY OF THE ORGANIZATION OF AMERICAN STATES.

November 3, 1966

The Director of Information of the Presidency of the Republic has the pleasure of presenting:

ADOLFO MENA

Special Envoy of the Organization of American States, who is undertaking a study and collecting information on the social and economic relations that prevail in the Bolivian countryside.

The undersigned, who has presented this credential, asks all national authorities and private persons and institutions to lend Señor Adolfo Mena all the cooperation that they can in order to facilitate his research effort.

signed:
Gonzalo Lopez,

Director of Information
Presidency of the Republic
La Paz, November 3, 1966

With Che carrying this document, Che and Pacho traveled from Cochabamba to the Ñancahuazú ranch in two separate jeeps, arriving there the night of November 6.

Che brought to Bolivia a contingent of seventeen Cubans. Most of the members of this hand-picked group were veterans of Che's guerrilla column in the Sierra Maestra. Six held the rank of *comandante* in the Cuban army. Many of them had served in important posts in the Cuban government, and several were members of the central committee of the Cuban Communist Party. All of these individuals were tied to Che by unquestioning personal loyalty. They were willing to follow him to hell if he asked them to do so, and in the end only three of them returned home to Cuba alive.

Che's Cuban comrades traveled to Bolivia in six separate groups. Like him, they all had excellent documents supporting their false identities. The first group arrived in Bolivia sometime in October, and the remaining five groups throughout November and December, the last group arriving at the ranch on December 19. Some entered Bolivia via the rail line from Arica, in nearby Chile. Others came by plane from São Paolo, Brazil. One group flew from Cuba to Prague, from there to Frankfurt, and from Frankfurt to La Paz via New York and Miami.

The Bolivian members of the guerrilla force were largely recruited by Coco and two other Bolivian agents, known by the code names of Rodolfo and Sánchez. The latter two men also served as a liaison between Che's group and the urban areas during the period before the guerrilla force was discovered. The entry in Che's diary at the end of November, 1966, indicates that he hoped to increase the number of Bolivians in his force to at least twenty before beginning military operations. In December he met with Mario Monje, the leader of the pro-Moscow Bolivian Communist Party, to discuss the possibility of receiving men and assistance from his party. However, Monje refused to support the guerrilla operation and Che was forced to recruit men from other sources. By the end of March, 1967, he had succeeded in recruiting approximately twenty Bolivians. A handful of these recruits were Bolivian students who had been trained in Cuba specifically for the purpose of fighting in the guerrilla operation. The remainder were dissident members of the young wing of Monje's party and unemployed miners from the tin-mining areas on Bolivia's high plateau.

The unemployed miners were recruited by Moises Guevara, an important union leader among the tin-miners in Oruro. Moises had traveled several times to Cuba and had met Che there on one of his visits. After Che failed to obtain the support of Monje's party, he asked Moises to join the guerrilla force with some of his miners. Moises agreed and brought eight men with him to the Ñancahuazú camp in February, 1967.

In addition to the Cubans and Bolivians, Che's guerrilla force included among its members three Peruvians known by the code names of El Chino, Negro, and Eustaquio. El Chino was supposed to establish Che's planned guerrilla *foco* in Peru. He brought Eustaquio, a radio operator, and Negro, a physician, to Che's camp during the latter part of February. They were to be joined later by an additional number of Peruvians who were supposed to train with Che's force.

The total number of combatants in the guerrilla force stood at forty-four when the first encounter between the army and Che's group took place in March, 1967. The composition of the guerrilla force at that time was as follows:

17	Cubans
22	Bolivians
3	Peruvians
2	Argentines (Che and Tania)
44	Total

Most of the leadership positions were held by Cubans. Che appointed his comrade Joaquín second-in-command of the guerrilla force and also leader of the rearguard. He also appointed Cubans to the posts of leader of the vanguard (initially Marcos and later Miguel), chief of operations (Alejandro), chief of services (Pombo), and chief of supplies (El Ñato). Inti and Coco were the only two Bolivians entrusted with any leadership responsibilities. Inti was placed in charge of finances and appointed political commissar to the Bolivians. Coco, who was initially placed in charge of urban contacts and recruitment, was later incorporated into the guerrilla force and assigned various responsibilities.

No additions to the guerrilla force took place after the outbreak of hostilities in March. Instead, the size of Che's force was steadily reduced as each encounter with the army took its toll. Che had hoped to recruit peasants from the local area once his force began operations, but he failed to recruit even a single peasant after the fighting began.

In November and December of 1966, the Cubans arrived at the ranch, and the first Bolivian recruits were brought by Coco and Rodolfo. During this time, the Bolivian called Bigotes acted as the operator of the ranch, while Che and his comrades established their camp in a densely wooded area some distance from the ranch house. Then, in twos and threes, Che and his men began exploring the Ñancahuazú River valley and the general area north of the ranch.

They soon discovered that the area they had chosen for their guerrilla *foco* was unlike anything they had expected. They found themselves in a hostile region characterized by innumerable deep and densely wooded ravines. The Ñancahuazú River twists its way through a very steep canyon. Along the river is a very narrow beach that occasionally disappears, forcing anyone along the river's edge to climb one of the steep walls on either side. This is extremely difficult because of the thickets which grow from the river's edge to the top of the ravine walls. These thickets are by far the worst enemy of man in the region. They are inhabited by clouds of voracious mosquitos and consist of thin reeds, twisting vines, and various cacti. The vines are so numerous in some places that it is impossible to see more than a few feet ahead. One of the more prevalent cactus plants in these thickets has large leaves with serrated edges. Anyone attempting to move through the thickets in which these plants abound can count on leaving some of his flesh and clothing behind. Injuries and accidents are common in this hostile terrain, and Che lost several of his men in fatal accidents before the fighting ever began.

In mid-December Che and his group moved farther away from the ranch house and deeper into the densely wooded area surrounding the Ñancahuazú River. There they established a second camp and spent the remainder of the month digging trenches and supply caves, building observation posts, cutting trails through the undergrowth surrounding the campsite, and practicing the defense of the area. Che also gave his men classes in guerrilla warfare and the political objectives of their operation. On January 6, for example, Che wrote in his diary that he had given the group that day a lecture on the qualities of the guerrilla soldier and had explained to his men that their mission was to form a nucleus of steel which would serve as an example for others to follow. The group also studied Quechua. This is an important Indian language in the highland areas of Bolivia and Peru, but it is of little use in the area where Che was planning to initiate his guerrilla operation.

In January, 1967, a number of serious problems emerged which were to vex Che and his group during the months ahead. First of all, they found themselves so short of food that it was necessary to send out regular hunting parties as well as to buy supplies in Lagunillas and Camiri. In addition, their neighbor Argañaraz told Bigotes that he "knew many things" and was willing to collaborate in "whatever they were doing." Thus it was clear that Argañaraz suspected something illegal was going on at the ranch and that he might inform the authorities. Che gave Bigotes instructions to accept Argañaraz's offer of collaboration, while at the same time threatening to kill him if he went to the authorities. Nevertheless, a few days later the ranch was visited by a Lieutenant Fernández and four policemen, who claimed they were looking for "the cocaine factory." The lieutenant made it clear to Bigotes that he expected to be bribed in return for permitting him to continue the cocaine factory. He took Bigotes' pistol and suggested that he come to Camiri in a few days, under the pretext of reclaiming his pistol, to discuss the whole matter. Following this visit, Bigotes and some of the others discovered that one of Argañaraz's men was spying on the ranch. They chased him away and established an observation post from which they could keep a close watch on Argañaraz. As if the problem of Argañaraz and the police was not enough, a number of Che's men fell sick with malaria, and the radio equipment was ruined by water seepage in the cave where it had been stored for safekeeping.

In view of the increasing possibility that the guerrilla force might be discovered by the authorities if it continued to remain at the ranch, Che decided to take his group on a training and reconnaissance march to the north. He had previously intended to undertake this exercise in mid-February, but the exigencies of the moment forced him to advance the date of departure to the first of February. Somewhat earlier, Che had instructed Tania to go to Argentina to interview his contacts there and bring them to the Ñancahuazú camp to discuss the possibility of establishing a guerrilla *foco* in the north of Argentina. Che had expected Tania to return with the Argentines before February, but when she did not arrive by February 1, he decided to start the march north without waiting for her. He left Bigotes and four men behind to watch over the ranch. They were instructed to meet Tania, the Peruvians, and Moises Guevara, who was due to bring his first group of recruits around the middle of February.

The morning of February 1, Che and his men left the ranch, heavily laden under their knapsacks and weapons. Their progress the first few days was painfully slow because of the constant rain and the fact that a number of the men, suffering from malaria, held the entire group back. They soon discovered that their maps of the area were incomplete and, in places, useless. On the sixth day, they reached the Rio Grande and had difficulty crossing it. Once having crossed the river, they encountered some peasants and attempted to win their sympathy by giving medical treatment to their children. But the peasants were suspicious of them and uncooperative.

During the next few weeks the guerrillas roamed across the broken terrain north of the Rio Grande, occasionally losing their way or encountering steep cliffs which forced them to double back over ground already covered. The difficult terrain, the heat, and their dwindling food supply began to affect their physical and psychological condition. By the end of the third week, Che himself was so exhausted that he was on the verge of collapse. On February 23, he wrote in his diary that he had made it on guts alone that day. He wrote that the sun was so hot at noon that it cracked stones, and that he nearly fainted climbing a hill. Che also noted that he had overheard Marcos, who was in charge of the vanguard, telling his comrades to go to hell.

A few days later, Marcos threatened Pocho with a machete. The incident was so serious that Che was forced to reprimand both of them before the entire group. He took the occasion to explain that the kind of physical discomfort they were experiencing was an introduction to what they could expect in the future, and that lack of discipline under such circumstances produced shameful incidents such as those which had occurred between the two Cubans. At the same time, he asked the Bolivians to be truthful and to tell him if they felt like quitting. He assured them they would be permitted to leave freely if their convictions weakened. Later the same day, one of the Bolivians, a young student named Benjamín, was forced to drop back behind the rest of the group because of exhaustion. As the remainder of the group was climbing a cliff alongside the Rio Grande, Benjamín strayed off the trail and fell into the river. He didn't know how to swim, and the current dragged him under almost immediately.

Although Che had planned to return to the Ñancahuazú camp by the first of March, the second week of March found his group still a long way from the camp and at the end of their food supplies. The scarcity of food seriously affected the morale of the group, and they soon became so weak they could make very little progress each day. Their preoccupation with their lack of food is evidenced by Che's diary notations for this period. They are very short and deal almost exclusively with whether or not any game was killed each day and how many rations they had remaining.

On March 14, they finally reached the Ñancahuazú River, which was very turbulent due to the heavy amount of rainfall which had occurred in the area the preceding weeks. Rolando, one of the best swimmers in the group, swam across the river and went on ahead to notify those at the camp that Che and the others would be arriving in a few days. However, it took Che three days to move the entire group and their equipment across the swollen river. A raft was built for this purpose, and on the last crossing another fatal accident ocurred. The raft was overturned by a whirlpool, and Carlos, one of the best of the Bolivian recruits, was lost in the swirling water, along with most of their ammunition.

The next day, the weary group resumed the march to the camp still some two days distant. In the afternoon Che and the others noticed a light airplane circling the area ahead of them. This alarmed Che considerably, particuarly since he had not received any news from the camp in many weeks. He decided to get to the camp as quickly as possible and told his exhausted column they would have to keep marching beyond nightfall. At about five thirty that evening they met the Peruvian named Negro, who had been sent by El Chino to find Che and tell him what had transpired in his absence. The news was upsetting. Two of the recruits recently brought to the camp by Moises Guevara had deserted, and the police had visited the ranch again.

At some point during the last two weeks of the march, Marcos and the vanguard had separated from the main force and gone ahead to the ranch. They evidently reached the ranch several days in advance of Che. As Che and his men approached the ranch, they encountered Pacho, who had been sent by Marcos with a message indicating that the situation was becoming increasingly critical. In addition to the two desertions and the police visit to the ranch, a large number of soldiers had moved into the area and had captured one of Moises Guevara's recruits. There was even some fear at this point that Bigotes had been taken prisoner as well.

During Che's long absence, a number of people had accumulated at the ranch. In mid-February, Coco had returned with Moises Guevara and his first group of recruits from the mines. They were followed by El Chino and his two comrades, Negro and Eustaquio. In addition, Tania came with several visitors. Only two of these visitors remained at the ranch to wait for Che's return. They were Regis Debray, the young French leftist writer, and Ciros Bustos, one of Che's Argentine contacts. This group had moved to a small campsite apart from the main base to wait for the return of Che and his men.

When Che arrived at the visitors' campsite, he found everyone there in a state of great confusion. The news that soldiers were in the area, that two of Moises Guevara's men had deserted, and that a third had been captured, had placed everyone's nerves on edge. Moreover, Che discovered that Marcos and the vanguard were not at the visitors' campsite or the main camp. In fact, as Che and his men reached the visitors' camp, one of the members of the vanguard arrived with instructions from Marcos to tell everyone in the camp to prepare for a complete withdrawal from the area. Che noted in his diary that there was an atmosphere of defeat and complete chaos among those present, and that no one appeared to know what to do.

Che immediately sent Marcos an angry message reminding him that "wars are won with bullets" and ordering him and the men with him to go at once to the main camp and defend it. In view of this situation, one wonders what would have happened if Che had not arrived at this moment. Marcos and the others would have withdrawn from the area and quite possibly fallen into an army ambush. Alternatively, Che and his group might have arrived at the camp to find it deserted. Unaware of the army's presence in the area, Che and his group might have then unsuspectingly run headlong into them. Indeed, it is difficult to understand how Che could have made the error of remaining away from the main camp for over a month and a half. In his absence something was sure to go wrong at the ranch, particularly in view of the arrival of a number of undisciplined new recruits.

Having ordered Marcos and the vanguard to the main camp, Che calmly spent the entire day of March 21 talking with El Chino, Debray, Bustos, and Tania. With El Chino he discussed the details of the Peruvian guerrilla *foco*. He agreed to give El Chino five thousand dollars monthly, provided he and his men took to the mountains in the Ayacucho region of Peru within six months. He next spoke to Debray, who indicated that he had come to join the guerrilla force. However, Che convinced him that he could do more for the guerrilla operation if he returned to France and organized international support for the Bolivian operation. Bustos made it clear he was willing to place himself at Che's disposal. Che therefore proposed that Bustos serve as a kind of co-ordinator of the Argentine contacts and make arrangements for the first five men from Argentina to be sent for training with the Bolivian group.

Tania told Che that she had contacted the right people in Argentina and brought them to the ranch. However, they had insisted she travel with them in their own jeep from Camiri to the ranch. Thus she was forced to leave her jeep parked on a side street in Camiri. But the Argentines, with the exception of Bustos, had left the camp and returned to Argentina when they discovered Che was not there. Tania decided to wait at the ranch for Che's return, since she was afraid her long absence from La Paz had created too much suspicion. As it was, the jeep which she had left parked in Camiri for several weeks did attract the attention of the police there, and upon investigation they discovered some documents in the jeep which later made it possible for them to link her to the guerrillas.

On March 22, Che moved everyone in the second campsite to the main camp, where Marcos and the vanguard were waiting. Upon arriving, he ordered Coco and five others to go down to the river and set up an ambush which would stop the soldiers if they attempted to approach the main camp from the river. He also sent several of his men on reconnaissance patrols in order to try and locate the exact position of the soldiers. Soon after Che's arrival at the main camp, Inti informed him that Marcos had treated him disrespectfully. Che became furious at Marcos and told him that if what Inti had reported was true, he could be expelled from the guerrilla force. Marcos, on the point of tears, answered that he would rather be shot than expelled from the group. However, the problem presented by Marcos' behavior was soon eclipsed by the news that a column of soldiers was marching in the direction of the guerrillas' camp.

CHAPTER 6

The Discovery of the Guerrillas and the Outbreak of Hostilities

⎍⎍⎍⎍⎍⎍⎍⎍⎍⎍⎍⎍⎍⎍⎍⎍⎍⎍⎍⎍⎍⎍⎍

On the morning of March 23, an army patrol led by Major Hernán Plata approached the guerrillas' main camp through the canyon of the Ñancahuazú River. The patrol, which was under orders to investigate the reported presence of Cuban-style guerrillas in the area, advanced along the river in three sections. The first section was led by Captain Emilio Silva, the second by Major Plata, and the third by Lieutenant Loayza. A fourth officer and a civilian guide, Epifano Vargas, accompanied the section led by Captain Silva. In all, there were approximately thirty soldiers. At about 7:00 A.M., Captain Silva discovered footprints near the river which led in the direction of the guerrilla camp. He halted the column and consulted with Major Plata. The major gave his consent to follow the footprints, and Captain Silva led the column up a path along one side of the river canyon. A few minutes later, the first section of the patrol approached the area where Coco and his men had set up their ambush. The guerrillas were positioned on both sides of the canyon so that they could catch anyone moving up the river in a crossfire.

As Captain Silva's section came within fifty feet of the guerrillas, the soldiers were startled by Coco's cry of "*Viva la liberación nacional*." Before the soldiers had time to react, they were caught in a rain of bullets. In a few minutes, the civilian guide Vargas, the officer accompanying him, and five soldiers lay dead along the path. The remainder of the first section, as well as the second section led by Major Plata, were hopelessly pinned down under the guerrillas' crossfire. Coco called on the soldiers to surrender. Seeing the futility of any resistance, Captain Silva ordered his men to cease firing and raise their hands. The men in Major Plata's section followed, while the third section, under Lieutenant Loayza, quicky retreated along the river.

As the smoke cleared, Coco and the other guerrillas in the ambush began collecting the soldiers' weapons and evaluating the results of the action. They counted seven dead, four wounded, and fourteen prisoners. Major Plata was found in a clump of bushes, suffering from a heart attack brought on by the shooting. He and the wounded soldiers were given medical attention by one of the Bolivian guerrillas who had formerly been a doctor. Coco ran back to the main camp to inform Che of the ambush and to ask for more men to guard the prisoners. He brought with him papers found on Major Plata which indicated the army's plan of operations. On the basis of this information, Che was able to ascertain that the army was advancing on the main camp from both extremes of the Ñancahuazú River and he was forewarned of the possibility of another patrol arriving at the rear of his camp from upriver.

Major Plata and Captain Silva were afraid they were going to be killed; Che's diary indicates that when Inti interrogated them, they "talked like parrots." According to Che, Major Plata said he was going to retire from the army, and Captain Silva claimed that he had reentered the army a year earlier at the request of "the

Party," implying that he was a Communist. He also said he had a brother studying in Cuba, and that he knew two officers who would be willing to collaborate with the guerrillas. Actually, Captain Silva was not a Communist and he did not have a brother studying in Cuba. He thought that if he could convince the guerrillas he was sympathetic to their cause he might save his life. Both he and Major Plata, therefore, were quite surprised when they learned the next day that the guerrillas were going to set them free and allow them to return unharmed to Lagunillas. They were also surprised by the cordial treatment they received. Of course, this was all part of Che's strategy. He hoped that such chivalrous treatment would earn the guerrillas the admiration of the soldiers and perhaps induce some of them to join the guerrilla force.

On March 24, approximately twenty-four hours after they had been captured, the soldiers were set free. Inti asked them first if they would like to join the guerrilla movement, and when they all refused, he ordered everyone but the officers to strip to their underwear. In exchange for their camouflage uniforms, they were given the olive-green fatigue pants and jackets of the guerrillas, and permitted to leave by the same trail they had been on when they were ambushed. That afternoon they reached the remainder of their unit and reported to the Fourth Army Division headquarters in Camiri what had transpired. Naturally, they exaggerated greatly the number of guerrillas who had captured them. Word was flashed to La Paz that perhaps as many as five hundred Castroite guerrillas were operating in the Ñancahuazú-Lagunillas region, and that an army patrol led by Major Plata had made contact with them near their main camp. It was in this manner that the news of the guerrillas' first and most successful military action was transmitted to the outside world, although at the time there was no official recognition of the fact that Che Guevara was the leader of the guerrilla operation.

Che's original plan was to begin military operations north of the Rio Grande and then slowly withdraw southward across a terrain carefully prepared with caches of arms and ammunition, food supplies, and fortified bases. He needed perhaps another month before this plan would have been ready to be put into operation. But he had to discard it when the army discovered his main base in the Ñancahuazú area. The army was able to do this because during the first few weeks of March it had received a number of credible reports about the presence of guerrillas in the Ñancahuazú area.

On the morning of March 11, two of Moises Guevara's new recruits left the main camp, ostensibly to go hunting. They took the path leading down to the river, but instead of going to the east, where the best hunting area was, they disappeared in the direction of Camiri. A few days later, they were arrested and brought to the headquarters of the Fourth Army Division in Camiri. There they gave their captors a detailed report concerning all they knew about the guerrilla operation.

They identified themselves as Vicente Rocabado and Pastor Barrera, both unemployed miners from the Oruro area. They said they had been recruited by the Communist union leader Moises Guevara to join a group in the southeast that was planning to launch a Cuban-type revolution in Bolivia. Because they were unemployed and Moises Guevara had promised them payment for their services, they said they agreed to join the guerrilla force. But after a month at the guerrillas' camp, where they claimed they were made to work as peons, they decided they were fed up with guerrilla life and would desert as soon as the first opportunity arose.

Rocabado and Barrera gave the army detailed information about the location of the guerrillas' camp, the number of people there, and the fact that most of the guerrilla force was away at the time on a training and reconnaissance march to the north. They said they had been told that Che Guevara was the leader of the operation and that he was with the others in the north. They also told their captors about the large number of Cubans in the guerrilla group and about the presence at the camp of Regis Debray, Ciro Bustos, and Tania.

The senior officers at the divisional headquarters in Camiri received this information with considerable skepticism, if not disbelief. "Guerrillas in Ñancahuazú, with Che Guevara as their leader? Impossible!" was the response of the divisional commander, Colonel Humberto Rocha, who thought it more likely that they were dealing with a gang of cocaine merchants or perhaps even a band of cattle thieves. But his skepticism was soon dispelled by the arrival at the divisional headquarters of Epifano Vargas, the oil-worker from Vallegrande.

Vargas told Colonel Rocha that he had encountered a number of men, clad in olive-green clothing and armed with automatic weapons, near the Ñancahuazú River around the 1st of March (this was undoubtedly Marcos and the vanguard). He said they had presented themselves to him as foreign geologists who were interested in buying food. Vargas had sold them some of his food and, because he suspected they were not geologists, had followed them at a safe distance until they reached the ranch. He then went directly to the army heaquarters in Camiri to report what he had seen. This report, together with the information given by the two deserters, prompted Colonel Rocha to dispatch troops to the Ñancahuazú ranch. He also ordered an immediate aerial surveillance of the entire zone. Vargas was asked to go along with the troops and serve as a guide. There is some evidence that he refused to go voluntarily and had to be taken along as a prisoner.

On March 16, units from the Fourth Division reached the ranch and seized the house and the portion of the ranch closest to the road. The next day, they captured Salustio Choque, one of Moises Guevara's recently arrived recruits. If the army had any doubts about the presence of guerrillas in the Ñancahuazú area, the capture of Choque erased them. He confirmed everything that Rocabado and Barrera had told the military authorities in Camiri. He also volunteered to guide the soldiers to the guerrilla camp. Major Plata's column apparently preferred to rely on Vargas instead of Choque as a guide, but Choque subsequently led another column, under Major Sánchez, to the guerrilla camp at the beginning of April. At that time, he showed them where the guerrillas had hidden their supplies, film, documents, and various other items of importance.

The information which Choque, the two deserters Rocabado and Barrera, and the oil-worker Vargas gave the Bolivian authorities led to the discovery and subsequent annihilation of Che's guerrilla force. This information enabled the army to locate Che's main base before his men were ready to begin military operations. It also gave the army the initiative from the beginning of the conflict until its tragic termination some six months later. Timing was a crucial factor in Che's strategy, and the premature initiation of hostilities threw his whole operation off-balance. His small force of men was never really able to recover from the shock of having the central base discovered before they were ready to begin fighting. All of Che's subsequent efforts were little more than valiant, but futile, attempts to put up a good fight in the face of overwhelming odds. He and his men seem to have deluded themselves during the first few months of fighting that their operation still could succeed, but in reality their fate was sealed from the beginning.

Che had written of the extreme danger which a guerrilla force faces during its preparatory stage in his article "Guerrilla Warfare: A Method." He pointed out that the future of a revolutionary movement depends upon the way in which the nuclear guerrilla force handles itself when the enemy moves against it. According to Che, unless the guerrillas are able to develop their capacity to attack the enemy during the early stage of the struggle, they have little prospect of surviving.

Regis Debray, in his work *Revolution in the Revolution?*, also noted that the crucial moment for a guerrilla force is the moment of its entry into action, and that here the question of timing is critical. Debray stated that the destruction of the guerrilla *foco* in its embryonic stage, before it has linked itself closely to the local population or gained sufficient experience, is the ideal accomplishment of any counterinsurgency operation. He went on to emphasize that once the guerrilla force had been discovered, it must not allow itself to be contained within a specific zone, for this deprives the guerrillas of their main weapon, mobility, and allows the regular army to utilize its forces most effectively. This was the precise situation in which Che's force found itself after March 23. As a result of the army's discovery of their main base, Che and his men were forced to withdraw into a relatively confined area. Whereas he had originally planned to have his force withdraw across a zone carefully prepared with caches of supplies and fortified bases, the army's discovery of their main base forced Che and his men to move into an area about which they knew very little and where they had difficulty finding food and places to hide.

Only Che's will to succeed and his refusal to accept defeat can explain his optimism about the future of his guerrilla operation after the discovery of his force in the Ñancahuazú area at the end of March. Anyone else undoubtedly would have concluded that under the circumstances there was no choice but to abandon the entire venture and escape while it was still possible to do so. But not Che; until the end he continued to believe that his movement would succeed. Perhaps he kept thinking of how high the odds had been against the success of Castro's operation after the *Granma* disaster, when only twelve members of the original eighty-man invasion force survived the landing on Cuban soil and made their way to the Sierra Maestra.

CHAPTER 7

The Capture of Regis Debray and Ciro Bustos

பாட்டப்பாட்டப்பாட்டப்பாட்டப்பாட்டப்பாட்டர்

Following their first clash with the army, the guerrillas were forced to withdraw from their main base in Ñancahuazú. As they moved north towards the little town of Gutiérrez, they discovered that there were a large number of troops stationed in the area immediately ahead of them. Che was forced to hastily modify his plans. Instead of heading north towards the Vallegrande region, he decided to make a diversionary move toward the south. By staging a surprise attack against the town of Muyupampa, some thirty miles to the southwest, Che reasoned that he and his men would have no trouble marching north along the series of ridges leading from the Muyupampa area toward the Rio Grande.

In addition to the shortage of food, the lack of preparation of his force, and the precariousness of their position, Che had the problem of slipping Regis Debray and Ciro Bustos out of the combat zone without their being captured by the Bolivian authorities. As previously mentioned, Che had convinced Debray that he would be of more value to the movement if he returned to France. As for Bustos, Che was depending on him to return to Argentina and lay the groundwork for the Argentine phase of the operation.

Faced with the difficulty of transporting them safely out of the area after the ambush of the army patrol on March 23, Che had initially offered Debray and Bustos three alternatives: (1) they could stay with the guerrilla force until a later date, when hopefully it would be easier for them to depart safely, (2) they could try to get out of the combat zone right away, or (3) they could stay with the guerrilla force until it reached Gutiérrez and from there take their chances at escaping. They chose the third alternative. But when they discovered that a large number of troops were defending Gutiérrez, they decided to accompany Che and the others to Muyupampa.

Not far from Muyupampa, Che's men captured an Anglo-Chilean reporter named George Roth, who had paid some youths in Lagunillas to lead him to the guerrilla force. Needless to say, Che was not happy to learn that the general location of his force was a matter of public knowledge in Lagunillas. On the other hand, Roth's arrival gave Debray an idea concerning how he and Bustos could leave the guerrilla force and get past the Bolivian authorities without arousing their suspicion. Both of them, pretending to be reporters, could leave in the company of Roth, and, if they were stopped, they could explain that all three of them had entered the area to interview the guerrillas.

Debray had entered the country legally, with credentials from the leftist Mexican magazine *Sucesos* and the Paris publishing house of Maspero. Therefore, he thought he would have no difficulty convincing the authorities that his presence in the area was legitimate. Bustos presented a problem, however, since he had entered the country with false documents and had no credentials that would support his contention that he was a journalist. Nevertheless, Debray persuaded Bustos that they would be able to con-

These photographs were taken from a roll of film found in the Ñanca-huazú camp. The top picture shows Che talking to several of his comrades. The woman standing behind the tree is Tania. *Below,* Che and some of the other guerrillas at the same campsite.

Bustos, El Chino, Che, and Debray in the Ñancahuazú cam

Some sketches of the guerrillas drawn by Bustos,
which were in his possession when he was captured.

The guerrillas' main camp in the Ñancahuazú area shortly after the Bolivian army took possession of it in April, 1967.

The adobe shack where Che's body was placed on display in Vallegrande.

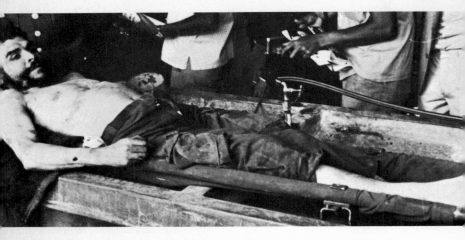

Che's body on display in Vallegrande.

Close-up of Che's face in death.

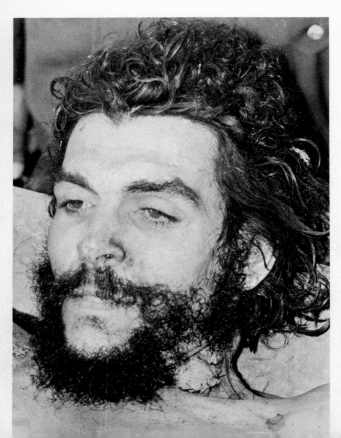

vince the Bolivian authorities that he was a fellow journalist if they were questioned. After consulting Bustos, Debray went to Che with his plan. Aware that there were as many troops around Muyupampa as in the Gutiérrez area, Che told Debray it would be better if they waited. But when Debray insisted on going and Bustos indicated he was willing to give the plan a try, Che reluctantly gave his consent.

Meanwhile, Roth was being held under guard a short distance from the main body of the guerrilla force, so that he would not discover that Che was the guerrillas' leader and that there were a large number of Cubans in the force. When Inti presented Debray's plan to Roth, he readily agreed to it. Roth not only thought the undertaking would provide him with an excellent story, but he was afraid of what might happen to him if he refused to help Debray and Bustos. Up until the point Inti presented Debray's plan to him, Roth had been afraid the guerrillas were not going to let him go. He knew that they were suspicious of him because his passport indicated he had spent some time in Puerto Rico, regarded by the guerrillas as the training ground for all U.S. agents in Latin America. Actually, Roth had been employed in Puerto Rico by the U.S. Peace Corps to teach Spanish to Peace Corps volunteers training there for assignments in Latin America.

On April 19, Debray and Bustos, together with Roth, left the guerrilla force just outside the town of Muyupampa. Debray had some last-minute doubts about leaving when he learned that Muyupampa was under heavy guard, but Bustos had made up his mind and Debray had no choice but to leave with him. Before they left, Che gave Debray a message which he was to deliver personally to Fidel. He also gave Bustos some money and final instructions regarding his mission to Argentina. A few hours later, the three were stopped and arrested by an army patrol on the outskirts of Muyupampa.

Since the Bolivian authorities had already been informed that a Frenchman and an Argentine were among the guerrillas, Debray and Bustos were immediately identified. At first, the Bolivians thought Roth was a guerrilla, but he was later released and allowed to return to Chile. On Bustos were found a series of sketches which he had drawn of the most important members of the guerrilla force, including Che. These proved very helpful to the Bolivian authorities in identifying many of the guerrillas.

The capture of Debray and Bustos gave the Bolivian government a propaganda field day. Above all, it provided them with visible proof of the "foreign" character of the guerrilla operation, and they did not fail to get as much mileage as possible out of this fact. They realized that in the eyes of most Bolivians they could effectively discredit the guerrillas by depicting them as foreign invaders intent upon intervening in the internal affairs of their country. Debray, in particular, was a perfect instrument for agitating and mobilizing the nationalistic sensibilities of the Bolivian people against the guerrillas. Not only was he a foreigner, he was also a well-known Marxist, a friend of Cuba, and the author of several works on revolution in Latin America, the latest being *Revolution in the Revolution?*, widely publicized as "a primer for Marxist insurrection in Latin America."

Soon after the capture of Debray and Bustos, the Bolivian government announced that both of them would be publicly tried by a military tribunal for their crimes against the Bolivian people. During the months preceding this trial, the government waged an intensive propaganda campaign against the prisoners, in particular Debray. When the trial was finally held during October, 1967, Debray was accused of a long list of crimes. According to the prosecutor, he had come to Bolivia as a spy on two previous occasions (he had visited the country several years earlier as a journalist). The prosecutor also accused him of bringing maps as well as money to the guerrillas, of being a member of the general staff of the guerrilla force, and of giving them training in guerrilla warfare. Finally, he claimed that Debray had personally participated in the guerrillas' ambush of the army column on March 23, and that he was the intellectual architect of the entire guerrilla operation.

Acting as his own attorney at the end of the trial, Debray made a brilliant, though perhaps too intellectual, defense of his actions. He argued that the government was pretending to condemn him for having performed a major role in the guerrilla operation, while in fact they were condemning him because he was a Marxist, an admirer of Fidel Castro and Che Guevara, and an advocate of revolution in Latin America. Debray said that if this was what he was to be punished for, he admitted to being guilty. But although he admitted his political and moral complicity, he reminded the tribunal that if they were going to continue with the pretext of trying him for violations of criminal law, then they could not condemn him for his beliefs or even his intentions, but only for whatever criminal acts they could prove he had committed. In this regard, he asserted that the government had failed to produce any evidence which proved that he had participated either directly or indirectly in the military activities of the guerrilla force. Furthermore, he claimed that Che's diary (introduced during the last part of the trial) supported his innocence in this respect.

Debray was correct about Che's diary. The journal in fact makes it quite clear that both he and Bustos were considered visitors, and that they did nothing more bellicose than occasionally take a turn at guard duty. To be sure, the diary also reveals that Debray asked Che for permission to join the guerrilla force as a combatant, and indicates that Che convinced him that he would be much more useful to the movement outside Bolivia. At the trial, Debray said that Che had also wanted him to leave because he was suffering from malnutrition and Che didn't have much confidence in his physical resistance. He claimed that Che alluded to his lack of experience and poor physical condition by telling him that one *campesino* was worth more to him than ten intellectuals from the city.

Che's diary also makes it quite clear that Debray was neither the intellectual architect of the guerrilla operation nor one of its planners. Che mentioned Debray's book, *Revolution in the Revolution?*, only twice throughout the twelve month-period covered in his diary. It is also clear from these references that Che had not read Debray's book until Debray himself gave him a copy to read in the guerrilla camp. At any rate, the book is based upon the revolutionary theories and practices of the leaders of the Cuban Revolution, in particular those formulated by Che. Therefore, it is hard to believe that Debray was the intellectual architect or that his book served as the primer for an operation organized and led by Che Guevara, one of the most prominent authorities on the theory and practice of revolutionary guerrilla warfare.

It seems that, apart from being caught trying to leave the guerrilla force, Debray never did anything more than serve as a messenger for the guerrillas. Che's diary reveals that he brought information with him from Cuba when he arrived at the guerrilla camp in March. However, this information had already been received by Che through other sources. Debray was subsequently instructed by Che to deliver a message to Fidel and, upon his return to France, to contact Jean-Paul Sartre and Bertrand Russell about organizing an international fund to help the Bolivian guerrilla movement. Actually, it was not Debray but Bustos to whom Che had given the responsibility of carrying out an important and truly subversive mission, i.e., that of laying the groundwork for an Argentine guerrilla *foco*.

It has been suggested that after he was captured, Debray gave the Bolivian intelligence service, as well as the CIA, information which they were able to use against Che and his guerrilla force. Indeed, it seems Che himself suspected that Debray and Bustos might have done this. In his diary entry on June 30, Che referred to having heard over the radio a declaration made by the head of the Bolivian armed forces, General Ovando, in which Ovando stated that Che was the leader of the guerrillas. Che noted that General Ovando had said his declaration was based on certain statements made by Debray. Che commented that it appeared Debray had said more than was necessary. Later, on July 10, Che wrote that the public statements made by both Debray and Bustos were not good, and he was especially upset that they had confessed the continental purpose of the guerrilla movement. At a press conference permitted by the army on July 9, Bustos did in fact tell reporters that Che was in Bolivia for the purpose of launching a revolutionary movement which would eventually encompass the entire continent. He also told them that Che had no more than forty or fifty guerrillas with him and that a number of them were foreigners. He specifically mentioned Coco and Inti Peredo as the two leading Bolivian members of the guerrilla force. The fact that Bustos' wife was allowed to visit him a few days after this interview, and that he later received better treatment than Debray, suggests that he may have made a deal with the Bolivian authorities.

In the case of Debray, it is quite possible that he unwillingly gave the CIA and the Bolivian intelligence authorities information about the guerrilla force. He obviously was very frightened after he was taken prisoner in Muyupampa. In the defense declaration made at his trial, he mentioned that he had been beaten by Bolivian intelligence agents after he was captured. Under the circumstances, he may have broken down and told the authorities everything. Moreover, at his trial he spoke of having been interrogated by a CIA agent who called himself Dr. Gonzales. According to Debray, Gonzales knew from the outset that he was not a guerrilla. Instead, he assumed that Debray had a confidential political mission to perform for the guerrillas outside of Bolivia. He questioned Debray about his mission, his relations with the Cuban government, the guerrilla movement's sources of support outside Bolivia, and, of course, about Che.

During the course of his testimony, Debray stated that he told Gonzales he had visited the guerrilla camp solely to interview Che but that upon arriving he had discovered that in fact a Bolivian named Inti was the guerrilla leader. But several weeks later, according to Debray, Gonzales returned with precise testimonies and detailed documents which proved beyond any doubt that Che was the leader of the guerrillas, and that Debray had "interviewed" him. At this point, Debray stated that he was forced to admit that he had interviewed Che and that he gave Gonzales a "summary" of this interview. What Debray really told Gonzales we can only guess. If he did give Gonzales any valuable information about Che and the guerrilla movement, he would now, of course, be ashamed to admit it.

Debray's motivation for going to Bolivia remains unclear. Did he go to the guerrilla camp so that he could write a sensational eyewitness account of Che's guerrilla operation in Bolivia, or did he go there in order to perfect his theories on revolutionary guerrilla warfare by directly participating in the operation? Perhaps his book, *Revolution in the Revolution?*, offers a partial answer. In it Debray wrote that ". . . the Latin American revolutionary war possesses highly special and profoundly distinct conditions of development, which can only be discovered through a particular experience." He argued that to understand this kind of war in the Latin American context it does no good to consult previous theoretical works on this subject. Instead, he used the analogy of learning a foreign language to support his point that this kind of war must be observed first hand. He stated: ". . . a foreign language is learned faster in a country where it must be spoken than at home studying a language manual." It would seem that Debray tried to follow his own advice by going to Bolivia to learn first-hand the "language" of revolutionary guerrilla warfare.

Why then was Debray so anxious to leave the guerrilla force so soon after he arrived? Did he perceive that Che's guerrilla operation was doomed to failure, did he become frightened for his own safety, or was he merely trying to relieve Che of the added problem of worrying about him and Bustos at a time when Che had more than enough to worry about? According to Debray, he felt that he and Bustos were greatly interfering with the mobility of the guerrilla force, particularly in view of his own bad health. He claims he insisted on leaving the guerrilla force as soon as the first opportunity arose, so as to reduce the burdens on Che. But if this was Debray's motivation for wanting to leave Che and the others, there is no evidence in Che's diary to substantiate it.

Che made no reference in his diary to Debray's having been ill. On the other hand, the diary suggests that Che suspected Debray was anxious to leave the guerrilla force because he was frightened. On March 28, for example, Che wrote that Debray was "too vehement about how useful he could be to the movement outside of Bolivia." Moreover, after Debray and Bustos had been captured and imprisoned, Che wrote that they were victims of "their own near desperation to leave the guerrilla force, and of his lack of energy to prevent them from doing so." He also noted that as a result of Bustos' and Debray's capture, his communication with Cuba was cut off, and his plan for establishing a guerrilla force in Argentina was lost.

Since Che's death, both Debray and Bustos have made a number of interesting statements about the failure of Che's guerrilla operation. Both of them appear to be living a rather comfortable existence in a former officer's club in Camiri, which has been converted into a special prison for them. According to reporters who have been allowed to visit them, they both admit that Che's guerrilla operation failed because of its lack of popular support and the betrayal of the pro-Moscow Communists.

In addition, Debray has confessed to reporters that he thinks the Bolivian government acted very intelligently in response to the guerrilla threat. Referring to the way in which the government used the people's sense of national pride against him and the guerrillas, he told Georgie Anne Geyer of the Chicago *Daily News* that "they made me the stranger. They put me in an untenable position. This thing of nationalism is very important. You cannot go beyond feelings of nationalism." He also claims that he has changed some of his ideas about revolution in Latin America. For example, in the same interview he said that he now feels that the armies of Latin America, including the Bolivian, present a major obstacle to revolution. In several other interviews, Debray has declared that the guerrilla operation led by Che was condemned to failure from the start. He claims that the CIA knew about the guerrilla operation in February, 1967, and that from that time forward the guerrillas were in an extremely precarious position.

Of the two, Bustos has made the most critical statements about Che and his guerrilla operation. He told Miss Geyer that "Che did everything wrong," and that "the biggest problem was Che's vision of the revolution as continental." Because of this, Bustos said, Che failed to see Bolivia in its proper perspective, and "he underestimated . . . the army, the [people's] will, and the nationalism." Bustos also criticized the number of Cubans Che brought with him to Bolivia, indicating that their presence tainted the entire undertaking.

What will happen to both Debray and Bustos now that the guerrillas have been eliminated and the fanfare has subsided is difficult to say. They may spend the next twenty to thirty years of their lives in a Bolivian prison. However, this does not seem very likely. The Bolivians have a reputation for being quite forgiving of their former political enemies after the heat of the moment has passed. Perhaps Debray and Bustos will be released after a few years. If so, it will be interesting to hear what they have to say at that time about their participation in the guerrilla operation and why it failed.

CHAPTER 8

The High Point of Guerrilla Activities

Throughout April, May, June, and July, the guerrillas foiled the army's efforts to trap and annihilate them. In fact, due to the ineptitude and inexperience of the Bolivian army, the guerrillas badly mauled some of the units sent out to encircle them and lost very few of their own men. Thus, they humiliated the army and embarrassed the government during the first months of the campaign.

Following their initial encounter with the army near their main camp on March 23, over two weeks passed before the guerrillas clashed with the army again. The second encounter took place on April 10 some twelve miles north of the guerrillas' main camp at a place along the Ñancahuazú River named Iripiti. On the morning of the tenth, the guerrillas were making their way toward the town of Gutiérrez by proceeding up the Ñancahuazú when they discovered that a patrol of fifteen soldiers was coming downriver. Che quickly ordered his men to set up an ambush on both sides of the river. A short time later, the soldiers arrived, and in the ensuing exchange of gunfire the lieutenant in charge of the patrol and two of his men were killed. Two soldiers were wounded and six more were taken prisoner, four managed to escape. On the guerrilla side there was only one casualty, the Cuban called El Rubio. He was found near the wounded soldiers with a bullet in his head and his jammed rifle and a grenade at his side.

The guerrillas learned from the prisoners that they were part of a company of soldiers currently in possession of the guerrillas' former main camp. Che calculated that the remainder of this company would most likely come in search of his group just as soon as the soldiers who had escaped the ambush reported back to their company commander. Therefore, he had his men establish another ambush and at around five that evening, a column of about forty-five soldiers under the command of Major Rubén Sánchez were caught in it. The first volley of gunfire killed the lieutenant, a sergeant, and several soldiers who were at the head of the column. The guerrillas called upon the remainder to surrender, but the Major ordered his men to keep shooting. However, since they could not see the guerrillas hidden in the thickets around them, it soon became obvious that the situation was hopeless, and Major Sánchez and most of his men surrendered. The rearguard of the column, accompanied by two reporters from La Paz, managed to escape the ambush and return to the army field headquarters in El Pincal, a few miles south of the guerrillas' former main base. The final results of this second ambush were seven killed, five wounded, and twenty-two soldiers taken prisoner (including the Major and several junior officers). The guerrillas suffered no casualties.

The wounded soldiers were cared for by the two doctors in Che's force, and Inti Peredo took charge of interrogating the prisoners. After the interrogation, the prisoners' rations and boots were taken and they were set free. The Major and his men, carrying their dead and wounded, walked some six miles on their bare feet before they finally reached their comrades. The news that the guerrillas had successfully ambushed the army twice on the same day, killing ten men and capturing more than thirty, was a source of considerable humiliation to the military high command.

Meanwhile, Che decided to divide his force into two groups. He appointed the Cuban called Joaquín (Juan Acuña Núñez, a member of the central committee of the Cuban Communist Party and one of the first *campesinos* to join Castro's guerrilla movement in the Sierra Maestra) as the leader of the second group. Joaquín's group consisted of fourteen persons, including those who were too ill to march at anything but a very slow pace, and the Bolivian recruits whom Che regarded as misfits. Among the sick were Tania and the Cuban called Alejandro, both of whom were suffering high fevers, plus Moises Guevara, who had recently been disabled by a gall bladder attack. Che wanted Joaquín to stay in the area immediately to the west of the Ñancahuazú River and make a demonstration there, while he and the second group, including Debray and Bustos, went to Muyupampa. It was from the soldiers taken prisoner in the Iripiti ambushes that Che had learned that the town of Gutiérrez was being used as a staging area by the army. This information led Che to forget Gutiérrez and march in the opposite direction to attack Muyupampa. After the raid on Muyupampa he hoped to rejoin Joaquín's group and then head north toward the Rio Grande. However, as Che and his group approached Muyupampa, they discovered that the town was under heavy guard and in a state of alert. Consequently, Che was again forced to change his plans, and, after dropping off Debray and Bustos, he and his group marched north toward the town of Ticucha.

On April 22, Che's group set up an ambush on the road running from the little village of Taperillas to Ticucha, some six miles further north. During the course of the day, the guerrillas stopped a small truck belonging to the government-owned petroleum company, also a considerable number of peasants, and another truck loaded with a large quantity of bananas. They confiscated the petroleum company truck and let the peasants go. At dusk a plane began to circle above their position, indicating that their presence had been detected. Nevertheless, they casually went about making the preparations for their departure and were still not ready to leave when they were surprised by shooting and the voices of troops calling upon them to surrender. According to the entry in Che's diary, at this point there was general confusion and a near panic among his men. However, they had already loaded their supplies and equipment into the small truck, and with the aid of this truck and six horses they managed to withdraw from the scene before they were encircled by the opposing troops. They could not find Loro, one of the Bolivian members of the guerrilla force, and left without him. They also left behind some merchandise which they had bought from the local inhabitants and a packet of U.S. dollar bills which fell from the bag of one of the Cuban guerrillas.

Having narrowly escaped encirclement by the army, Che's group moved north of Ticucha to a place called El Mesón, where they established camp and waited for Joaquín's group. But on April 25, a column of sixty soldiers arrived in the area. The guerillas had very little advance warning of their approach, and they were forced to set up a hastily improvised ambush along the path leading to their camp. Much to the surprise of Che and his men, the advance element of the army column was led by a soldier with three trained German shepherds. As the dogs excitedly advanced into the ambush area, Che shot at the first dog and missed; he was about to shoot at the soldier guiding the dogs when his carbine jammed. One of Che's comrades shot the guide and a dog, but this warned the rest of the approaching column, and they did not fall into the ambush. As they withdrew down the road, the soldiers exchanged shots with a group of the guerrillas. When the shooting stopped, Che sent one of his men to tell this group to withdraw from the area; he learned then that one of his Cuban comrades, Rolando, had been fatally wounded.

Rolando, whose real name was Eliseo Reyes Rodríguez, had joined Castro's guerrilla force at the age of sixteen and had been promoted to the rank of captain during Che's famous march from the Sierra Maestra to Las Villas. He was a member of the central committee of the Cuban Communist Party and one of Che's closest companions. His death was a heavy blow to Che, who had intended placing him in charge of an eventual second front. In his diary, Che wrote that he had lost his best man, one of the pillars of the guerrilla force, and his comrade from the time he was a messenger in his column in the Sierra Maestra.

Because the army had discovered their location, Che and his men were forced to withdraw from the area where Joaquín's group was supposed to join them. Instead of heading north toward the Río Grande, they worked their way back towards the Ñancahuazú River in hopes that they might encounter Joaquín and his companions. Low on food and uncertain of the terrain, they traversed the rugged hills and ravines between El Mesón and the Ñancahuazú. At the end of April, Che wrote in his diary that it had been a month in which "everything was resolved normally," taking into consideration "the necessary eventualities of the guerrilla operation." Yet he also noted that their isolation was complete, that they had lost contact with Joaquín's group, and that they had done nothing to build a base of peasant support. In addition, he had to admit that the capture of Debray and Bustos had cut off his communication with Cuba and ruined his plans for preparing a guerrilla operation in northern Argentina. However, he seems to have been encouraged by radio reports that U.S. military advisors had been sent to help the Bolivian army. He believed that the United States would soon be forced to intervene with its own troops, thereby turning Bolivia into another Vietnam.

During the first week of May, Che and his comrades traversed the area north of their former main base, hoping to encounter Joaquín and the others. On May 7, they arrived at one of the small campsites along the Ñancahuazú, where they had buried some ammunition and supplies. Although it was apparent that the army had visited the campsite sometime before their arrival, their cache had not been discovered. The guerrillas spent the night at the campsite eating the small amount of food they had left. The next morning they captured four soldiers who stumbled into the area. That same day, a small patrol came down the river and the guerrillas ambushed them, killing the lieutenant in charge and two soldiers, and capturing six more soldiers. The guerrillas ate what little food they found on the soldiers and supplemented this with some lard they had stored in the supply caves. On the morning of May 9, the guerrillas lectured the soldiers and set them free, minus their shoes and uniforms. Shortly thereafter, Che and his men withdrew from the area and headed upriver. Since they had no other food, they were forced to eat lard soup that night, and many of the men became quite sick.

On May 12, the guerrillas came upon a small farm and feasted on pork, roasted squash, and husked corn, which they obtained from the local peasants. They departed that evening with almost every member of the group sick. The next day, Che made the following entry in his diary: "A day of belching, farting, vomiting, and diarrhea, a veritable organ concert. We remained absolutely immobile trying to digest the pork." On May 16, Che was overcome by an attack of vomiting and diarrhea so violent that he lost consciousness and had to be carried in a hammock. He wrote in his diary that when he awoke he felt quite relieved, but because he had no water to clean himself, his stench extended for at least a full league. Throughout the next week, Che and his men kept on the move and, apart from capturing a few peasants, they did not engage in any military action.

On May 28, Che and his men took control of the small town of Caraguataenda. They stationed themselves at either end of the town and confiscated two vehicles belonging to the government petroleum company and two which were privately owned. That evening, they drove these vehicles to the neighboring town of Ipitacito, where they broke open a store and took some merchandise. As payment for the items they had taken, they left behind five hundred dollars in U.S. currency and a rather ceremonious affidavit. From Ipitacito they traveled to the town of Espino, which is situated near the railroad that runs from Santa Cruz south to the Argentine border. Che at first planned to go from Espino toward the Rio Grande, but later changed his mind and decided to follow the road leading north from Espino to the town of Muchiri, where there was plenty of water.

On May 30, the guerrillas started for Muchiri, but they soon discovered that they had chosen the wrong road. Consequently, Che established an ambush along the road and sent out exploring parties to ascertain which direction they should follow. At about three o'clock, a column of soldiers preceded by a truck came toward the ambush. The guerrillas opened fire, forcing them to withdraw. An officer and a soldier were killed, and four were wounded. When Che was sure that the army had retreated, he ordered his men to leave the ambush area.

The guerrillas were forced to abandon all the vehicles confiscated in Caraguataenda, except one jeep; the others had run out of gasoline or water. By urinating into the radiator of the jeep and adding a few canteens of water, they were able to drive it north toward Muchiri. The next day, they discovered that the dusty road they had been following came to an abrupt end. They detained a peasant on a side road and asked him where they could find water and roads out of the area. With the peasant as their guide, Che sent a group of his men out to look for water and food. On the way, they saw two army trucks and hastily established an ambush. They partially destroyed one of the trucks with a grenade and wounded two soldiers. When they reported back to Che, he ordered everyone to resume the march. They advanced another nine miles, but during the course of this march the jeep ran out of gasoline and they were forced to leave it behind. That night, Che wrote his summary of the month, in which he indicated that he was encouraged by the military actions of his group but worried about their lack of contact not only with Joaquín's group but with La Paz and Cuba. He also mentioned that they had as yet failed to incorporate a single peasant into their movement. With Joaquín's group absent, he noted, his force consisted of only twenty-five men.

It is difficult to say with any certainty where Joaquín and his companions were during this period. Che thought they had moved north of the Rio Grande, but it appears that they were well hidden somewhere in the Ñancahuazú area. At any rate, they successfully avoided contact with the army during April, May, and June.

On June 1, several aircraft circled the area through which Che and his men were moving, but they apparently did not sight the guerrillas, who continued their march without encountering any soldiers. On June 2, Che and his men reached a farm, where they took a large pig and forced the farmhands to serve as their guides. While they were following an arroyo running alongside a road, an army truck passed carrying two soldiers and some barrels. It was an easy target, but Che let it go by and they continued on their way. They spent the night cooking and eating the pig, and afterwards released the peasants, paying them each ten dollars for the inconvenience. The following day they established an ambush along the road, and the same army truck which they had let pass the day before came down the road again. As before, there were two very cold-looking soldiers wrapped in blankets and riding in the rear of the truck. In fact they looked so pitiful to Che that he let the truck pass through the ambush unmolested. Later, he wrote in his diary that he did not have the heart to shoot at them and didn't think fast enough of the possibility of detaining them. The guerrillas gave up the ambush that evening without having caught a single military vehicle. For the next few days they hiked overland until they reached the banks of the Rio Grande, just below the village of Puerto Camacho. From there they slowly worked their way east along the south bank of the river.

Che and his men reached a point along the river on June 9 which required that they either cross to the other bank or leave the river and trek through thickets and ravines. They decided to cross the river. However, their efforts to build a raft failed, and Che sent a small party out to find a boat. A short time later, this group was sighted by a detachment of troops on the other side of the river, who began shooting at the guerrillas with mortars and small arms. The guerrillas exchanged some shots with the soldiers and then returned to where Che and the others were anxiously waiting. Instead of withdrawing from the area, Che ordered his men to establish an ambush if the soldiers attempted to cross the river. Meanwhile, he had a couple of his men cut a trail so that they could get out of the area without crossing the river. The army failed to advance, and the guerrillas left the area the next day by way of the new trail.

For several days, the guerrillas headed east parallel to the Rio

Grande. On June 16, they crossed the river and continued east past the town of Abapo. On the way, they took as prisoners three men they thought were traders. Later, near Abapo, they encountered a peasant boy named Paulino, who informed them that the three prisoners were in fact working for the army. Although Che considered killing the three, he decided to turn them loose with a severe warning and without their pants. Paulino said he was willing to help the guerrillas and promised them he would travel to Cochabamba to deliver several messages for them, including a coded letter to be sent to Cuba. But he was caught shortly after leaving the guerrillas.

The guerrillas headed north toward the town of Florida, and on June 26, Che had his men establish an ambush on the road leading to this town. Later in the day a column of soldiers fell into his trap; when they withdrew, they left behind four of their men dead. Che evidently assumed they would not counterattack and he did not order his men to evacuate the area. As it grew dark, however, the guerrillas came under heavy fire from the soldiers and were forced to retreat. In the withdrawal, two of the Cubans, Pombo and Tuma, were wounded. Pombo was only slightly wounded in the leg, but Tuma died a few hours later.

Tuma's death was a great personal loss for Che. He wrote in his diary that Tuma had been his inseparable and loyal comrade throughout the preceding years, and that he had come to regard him almost like a son. As an expression of his affection for his fallen comrade, Che personally buried Tuma, and he was still grieving over Tuma's death several days later when he called his men together for a general discussion in which he explained what the loss of Tuma meant to him personally. Moreover, in his monthly summary, he noted that the loss of each of his men amounted to a grave defeat, although the army did not realize it.

From the town of Florida, Che and his men continued north toward the main highway that runs between Santa Cruz and Cochabamba. Che's asthma seems to have become a constant source of discomfort during this time. Nevertheless, on the night of July 6 he led his men in the most daring action of the entire guerrilla operation. That night, they stationed themselves along the highway near a place called Peña Colorada. Che's plan was to stop a vehicle coming from the town of Samaipata, a few miles to the west, and find out from the driver how well-guarded the town was. But, after waiting in vain for a vehicle to come from the direction of Samaipata, Che had Coco, El Chino, and several of the Cubans stop a truck coming from Santa Cruz and drive it into Samaipata. When they reached the town, they immediately captured two policemen and then took the town's small army post after an exchange of gunfire with one of the soldiers on guard. Having captured the post, they transported the lieutenant in charge, along with the ten soldiers under his command, to a place some distance from the town and left them naked in the dark. They also raided the local pharmacy but failed to bring back the type of medicine which Che needed for his asthma. The entire foray was carried out in view of a large number of spectators, and the news of this raid, so close to the city of Santa Cruz, shocked the country, and particularly the government. It was only after this action that the army began an all-out effort to eliminate the guerrillas.

Following the raid on Samaipata, Che and his men withdrew south, almost retracing the route which they had taken from the Rio Grande to Samaipata. During this period, Che's asthma steadily grew worse and a decision was made to return to the Ñancahuazú area in order to get medicine for him from the supply caves. On July 12, Che heard over the radio that the army had clashed the day before with a group of guerrillas in the Ñancahuazú area, killing one of the guerrillas and taking his body to Lagunillas. The report was based upon an encounter between Joaquín's group and the new army units sent into the Ñancahuazú area as part of the army's "operation Cynthia," the government's answer to the Samaipata raid. On July 9, the hiding place of Joaquín's group had been discovered by the army. Joaquín and his companions managed to flee before they were surrounded, but they were forced to leave behind a large quantity of their supplies and possessions. When the army arrived, the found a number of documents, photographs, a code book, and a list of the members of Joaquín's group. On the following day, the army almost encircled Joaquín's group again and in the encounter killed one of the Bolivian members of the group.

Meanwhile, following the Samaipata raid, Che's group avoided contact with the army until July 27. By then they had moved south, past the town of Florida, on their way to the Rosita River, which runs into the Rio Grande. On this date, they caught a small reconnaissance patrol of eight soldiers in an ambush which they had set up just outside the village of Moroco. Three soldiers were killed and a fourth was wounded. They continued moving south, and on the night of July 29 they camped next to the Suspiro River. Just before dawn the next morning, they were surprised by a company of soldiers, who had stumbled upon their camp. There was general confusion on both sides, and in the darkness Che and his men withdrew across the river. However, in the prevailing confusion, eleven of their knapsacks were left behind, along with some medicine, binoculars, a tape recorder (which they used to record coded messages from Cuba disguised as part of the regular short-wave broadcasts of Radio Havana), and Che's personal copy of Debray's *Revolution in the Revolution?*, containing his own notes. Worse yet, in the withdrawal across the river, three of Che's men were shot. Two of them, the Bolivian called Raul and the Cuban named Ricardo, were fatally wounded, while the third, Pacho, suffered only a slight wound. The army suffered three dead and six wounded.

Che was very disturbed by this encounter. However, he doesn't seem to have grieved as much over the loss of Raul and Ricardo as he did over that of Tuma and Rolando. In his diary, Che referred to Ricardo as the most undisciplined member of the Cuban contingent, but acknowledged that he had been an extraordinary fighter and an old comrade from the campaigns in Cuba and the Congo. Of Raul, he had little good to say, admitting that he was neither much of a fighter nor much of a worker.

On the other hand, the reduction of his force to twenty-two members, and the fact that three of this number (including himself) were "crippled" (in his case by asthma), was a matter of some concern to Che. He was also upset about the mistakes his group had made in the last encounter with the army, particularly the fact that they had been surprised and forced to leave behind a good deal of their equipment and personal possessions. Che knew that the army's capture of these items would give the government a tremendous propaganda victory and greatly increase the morale of their troops. Although he did not state it in so many words, it is obvious from the monthly summary in his diary at the end of July that he recognized the guerrilla's situation had worsened considerably from that of previous months. He noted their failure to make contact with La Paz and Cuba through the peasant boy Paulino, and their continued lack of support from the peasantry. He wrote that their most urgent needs were to reestablish contact with the outside and to recruit more men. In addition, he noted that *his* most urgent need was to obtain medicine for his asthma.

CHAPTER 9

The End Nears

Throughout the first week of August, Che's group slowly worked their way southwest toward the Rio Grande. On August 8, Che decided he could no longer do without medicine for his asthma; he decided to send several men ahead to the supply caves in the Ñancahuazú area to bring some back. That night, he brought everyone together and informed them that in his present condition he was little more than a human carcass and that the situation facing them was one of those in which great decisions have to be made. He then told his comrades that the struggle in which they were involved offered them the opportunity to convert themselves into true revolutionaries, which he characterized as the highest level of the human species, and the chance to become men. He made it clear that those who felt they could not attain either of these states should say so and leave the struggle. Afterwards, Che wrote in his diary that "all the Cubans and some of the Bolivians stated they would continue until the end." He also noted that this was followed by a discussion in which several members of the group criticized each other regarding petty matters, and he was forced to end the meeting by telling them that such bickering took the greatness out of the decision they had made.

Che's condition became so bad after the departure of the group sent to fetch his medicine that he was forced to ride on one of the pack mules that had been bought from some peasants several weeks earlier. (As the days passed, the guerrillas were forced to eat these mules.) On August 12, Che was disturbed by a radio announcement that claimed the army had killed a guerrilla and discovered two deposits of arms and ammunition in the Ñancahuazú area. Actually, this report referred to the clash between the army and Joaquín's group that had taken place on August 10. In this encounter, the army shot the Bolivian guerrilla called Pedro (a former university student from the Cochabamba area) while he was covering the retreat of Joaquín and the others. The army was extremely proud of their performance in this encounter; they had carried off their entire action without a single soldier being killed or wounded.

Worse news was yet to come. Following this encounter, the army captured two of the Bolivian members of Joaquín's column, Chingolo and Eusebio. The prisoners told their captors everything they knew and then led a column of soldiers to the supply caves where the guerrillas had hidden, among other things, Che's medicine, all kinds of documents, and various rolls of undeveloped photographs. When Che heard the radio announcement concerning the discovery of these caves, he was terribly shaken. He wrote in his diary: "Now I am condemned to suffer asthma for an indefinite period. They have also taken documents of all types and photographs. It is the hardest blow they have given us; someone talked. Who? This is the mystery."

Since it was too late to send word to the group that had been sent ahead to obtain his medicine, Che and the men with him continued to the Rio Grande, intending to wait there for the others to return. Che's group reached the north bank of the Rio Grande on the evening of August 17, after considerable delay and difficulty. The following day they crossed the river and headed west along its south bank. That night, Che received the first indication that some of the Bolivian members of his force wanted to resign. Inti informed him that the guerrilla called Camba had told him privately that he wanted to leave the guerrilla band; Camba claimed his physical condition would not allow him to continue, and besides, he did not see any future in the struggle. Che wrote in his diary that Camba's case was a typical one of cowardice, and that it would be best to let him go. However, since Camba knew of their plans to try and find Joaquín and his group, Che decided that they could not afford to let him leave yet. The next day, Che explained this to Camba and also talked with his companion, Chapaco, who told Che he wanted some hope of being able to leave the guerrilla force within six months to a year. Che noted in his diary that Chapaco did not seem well, and that he had talked in a confused manner about a series of disconnected subjects.

On August 24, Che's group was heading west along the north bank of the Rio Grande when they spotted three men on the other side of the river. They immediately took positions for an ambush, and soon eight soldiers appeared. Che instructed his men to let the soldiers cross the river by way of the ford in front of them and then to shoot them as they approached the ambush. However, the soldiers did not cross the river. Instead, they walked off in the opposite direction. The next day, the same thing happened. Seven soldiers appeared on the opposite bank of the river but did not attempt to cross. Shortly afterwards, Che wrote in his diary that Camba had reached the ultimate point of moral degradation, since he had begun to tremble at even the mention of soldiers.

The same seven soldiers returned on August 26, but this time two crossed the river while the remainder stayed on the other side. The Cuban called Antonio, whom Che had placed in charge of the ambush, shot at the two soldiers too soon and missed both of them. They escaped and, together with their comrades, withdrew from the area on the run. Inti and Coco ran after them but the soldiers took cover and began shooting, forcing them to give up the chase. Meanwhile, Che noticed that bullets coming from the direction of his own men were hitting the area around Coco and Inti. He ran to the ambush and found Eustaquio shooting in their direction because Antonio had failed to give him any orders. Che was so angered by this that he lost control of himself and manhandled Antonio.

In a short time, the soldiers returned with reinforcements, but Che decided to withdraw from the area, and the soldiers did not pursue them. August 27 was spent in a desperate search for a way out of the rugged area into which they had withdrawn. However, the day was brightened by the appearance of the men Che had sent to the Ñancahuazú supply caves. After a long trek, during which they had barely escaped capture several times, they had heard the shooting between Che's group and the soldiers the day before. They then located Che and his men by following their tracks from the river.

Che and his force spent the remaining days of August slowly making their way through the dense thickets and rugged terrain somewhat to the north of the Rio Grande. Although they had expected to find water in the area, they did not, and on August 29, Che wrote that Chapaco, Eustaquio, and El Chino were on the verge of collapsing from thirst. The next day, he reported that the men he had sent ahead to cut a path through the thickets were suffering from fainting spells and that several of the others were drinking their own urine. However, later in the day they finally discovered some water, and with renewed strength they spent the last day of the month scaling the last ridge between them and the Rio Grande.

In his summary for August, Che wrote that it had undoubtedly been their worst month since the war began. He concluded by noting that the morale and revolutionary legend of his force had reached a low point, and that their most urgent tasks were to reestablish contact with the outside world, to incorporate new members, and to obtain medicine and supplies. The only optimistic note in the diary entry was that Inti and Coco were becoming increasingly outstanding soldiers and revolutionaries.

Several days later Che learned that Joaquín's column had been wiped out in an army ambush on August 30. Ironically, his column was ambushed no more than a day's march from where Che and his men were located. Apparently, Joaquín and his comrades were heading toward the area where they assumed Che and his group were operating; their decision to cross the Rio Grande in order to rejoin Che and the others turned out to be a tragic mistake.

In preparation for their journey to find Che's group, Joaquín and his companions had bought a cow from a peasant named Honorato Rojas. They had asked Rojas where the best place was to cross the Rio Grande and he had told them of a ford, called El Vado del Yeso, where it was possible to wade across the river. Confiding in Rojas had been a fatal mistake, for the day following their encounter with him a column of thirty soldiers under the command of Captain Mario Vargas visited his house. Rojas told Vargas that the guerrillas were probably going to cross the Rio Grande at El Vado del Yeso that very day. Vargas and his column headed immediately in the direction of El Vado del Yeso. Along the way, they encountered two peasants who had been taken prisoner by Joaquín's group the day before but had managed to escape the guerrillas' camp just a few hours earlier. With the peasants as their guides, Vargas and his men set up an ambush across from where the guerrillas were expected to ford the river.

The soldiers waited impatiently for the guerrillas to arrive. Finally, at about six o'clock in the evening, the Cuban named Braulio appeared out of the brush across the river. As he walked to the bank of the river, some of Captain Vargas' men asked permission to open fire, but he told them to hold their fire until all the guerrillas were clearly visible. As the soldiers waited, Braulio signaled to his comrades and they appeared from the brush one at a time. They began crossing the river in single file, with Joaquín in the lead and Tania at the rear. When the majority of the guerrillas were in the water, Vargas gave the order to commence firing. As the first shots hit the water around the guerrillas, they threw off their knapsacks and tried to escape in the river. They scattered, forcing Vargas and his men to leave their positions. They ran along the banks of the river shooting at the guerrillas still in the water as well as those trying to escape into the brush. Within twenty minutes, the soldiers had liquidated Joaquin's column, killing everyone but the Bolivian named Paco (his real name was José Carrillo), who was wounded and later taken prisoner.

Tania was one of the first to fall. Dressed in a white blouse and brown pants, in sharp contrast to her fatigue-clad comrades, she was a perfect target in the evening twilight. She was shot before she ever had a chance to throw off her knapsack or use her rifle. Her body was carried some distance down river by the current, and was not found until several days after the ambush. Meanwhile, the remains of her comrades were taken to the town of Vallegrande, where they were inspected by the press and high military officials. Among the bodies laid out for inspection were those of the former Bolivian miners' union leader Moises Guevara and the Peruvian called El Negro. A short time earlier, Bustos had been taken from his cell in Camiri to a location near El Vado del Yeso so that he could identify certain of the guerrillas. When Tania's body was brought to Vallegrande, President Barrientos was in the town on an inspection tour of the combat zone. He was pleased by the events of the last few days and told reporters that the remaining guerrillas operating in the zone would be promptly exterminated. He also offered amnesty to any Bolivian member of the guerrilla force who was willing to surrender. A few days later, Barrientos announced that the government would give fifty thousand Bolivian pesos (forty-two thousand American dollars) for the capture of Che Guevara dead or alive.

Although Che heard a broadcast by the Voice of America on September 2 which announced that a group of ten guerrillas led by a Cuban called Joaquín had been liquidated by the Bolivian army in "the zone of Camiri" three days earlier, he refused to believe it and similar announcements broadcast subsequently. It was not until the end of September that he finally admitted that the news about Joaquín's group was true. Even then, he thought there might still be a few members of Joaquín's column who had escaped the ambush and were avoiding contact with the army.

On September 3, at a place near the Rio Grande called Masicuri Bajo, a small group of Che's men clashed with a unit of forty soldiers while on a mission to purchase food from the local peasants.

The soldiers surrounded the guerrillas but for some unaccountable reason they then retreated instead of closing in on them. In the confusion, the guerrillas killed one of the soldiers and escaped without any casualties. However, they were forced to return without any food. The next day, Che sent out a second group under the command of Inti, with instructions to obtain food and to capture a soldier if it was possible to do so without risking losses. On September 5, they returned with a mule and some food, but without a prisoner. On the following day, Che had eight of his men establish an ambush along the path by which Inti and the others had returned to the camp, in case the army followed their tracks. Late that night, Che sent a man to tell the ambushers to rejoin the rest of the group. On his way, the messenger ran into an army patrol. The shots fired by the soldiers warned the men in the ambush as well as those with Che. Consequently, in the darkness, both groups were able to link up and withdraw from the area unharmed. As they left, they heard prolonged gunfire behind them as the soldiers fired aimlessly into the darkness.

On September 7, Che heard over the radio that Paco (the only survivor of Joaquín's group) had given valuable information to the army concerning the guerrilla movement and Debray's participation in it. Che was incensed over Paco's conduct and wrote in his diary that "he would have to be punished as an example." How Che thought he could punish Paco is a mystery, and one wonders what state of mind Che was in when he wrote this. The next day, Che heard that President Barrientos had been present at Tania's burial, and that a Communist newspaper in Budapest had criticized Che as a pathetic and irresponsible figure. This last announcement prompted Che to write in his diary that he would like to seize power if only to unmask cowards and lackeys of all species and rub their noses in their own dirt.

Following their brush with the army on September 6, Che and his men headed in a northwesterly direction away from the Rio Grande toward the town of Alto Seco. During the next week they were forced to climb an almost unending series of rugged hills and ford several swollen streams and small rivers. This march cost them equipment, lost in one of the streams, and weakened them both physically and mentally. On September 15, they were jolted by a radio broadcast which announced that sixteen members of their underground network in La Paz had been arrested, among them a young girl named Loyola Guzmán. Loyola had visited the guerrillas' main base prior to the outbreak of hostilities, and had been photographed with Inti and Coco on the very film that was discovered many months later in the supply caves near the guerrillas' former main base. It was these captured photographs which led the Bolivian authorities to Loyola, and from her to most of the guerrillas' handful of contacts and supporters in La Paz. In fact, the Bolivian authorities found a lot of valuable information in Loyola's house, including a list of all of Che's urban contacts.

Loyola tried to commit suicide while she was being interrogated in the Ministry of Interior by jumping out of a third-floor window, but her fall was broken by a cornice of the building and she was only slightly injured. After the police took her to the hospital, she told the press that she had wanted to kill herself because she had betrayed her comrades.

The news of Loyola's arrest and the police roundup of suspected guerrilla contacts in La Paz appears to have had a demoralizing effect on many of Che's men. On September 16, there was an altercation between the Bolivian called Chapaco and Antonio, one of the Cubans. And that night, the Peruvian Eustaquio accused one of the Bolivians of having eaten an extra meal. Moreover, two days later Chapaco staged a scene in which he accused a Cuban, Arturo, of having stolen fifteen bullets from his magazine, and Benigno, another Cuban, of having committed the error of allowing some peasants to see him and then leave the area freely. When Che learned this, he furiously called Benigno's error an act of treason. Che's angry rebuke hurt Benigno deeply, and he broke down crying.

On September 22, Che and his men arrived at the village of Alto Seco, where they discovered that the mayor had learned they were coming and had left to inform the army. Nevertheless, the guerrillas spent the rest of the day there and that evening Inti Peredo gave a lecture on the objectives of the guerrilla movement to an audience of fifteen dumbfounded villagers in the local school-house. Later that night, after purchasing a considerable quantity of food from the frightened inhabitants of Alto Seco, the guerrillas left, heading toward a nearby ranch called Loma Larga. On September 24 they arrived at the ranch exhausted and sick. Che reported in his diary that all but one of the peasants in the area had fled upon their arrival.

Two mornings later, when Che and his men reached the village of La Higuera, they noticed that something was wrong: all the men were gone and there were only a few women in the village. Coco went to the telegraph office and discovered there a telegram from Vallegrande informing the mayor of La Higuera that the guerillas were in the zone and that any information about them should be sent to the sub-prefect in Vallegrande. The guerrillas questioned the few people left in the village, who nervously explained that most of the inhabitants were attending a celebration in the nearby town of Jahue.

At one o'clock, Che ordered the vanguard of his force to leave for Jahue, but about a half hour later he heard shots coming from the road which they had taken. Fearing the worst, he ordered the remainder of his men to take up defensive positions in the village. A few minutes later, Benigno arrived, wounded, followed by Aniceto and Pablito, whose foot was in bad shape. They informed Che that they had fallen into an army ambush just outside the village and that Coco Peredo and the Cubans Miguel and Julio had been killed. As for Camba, he had disappeared when the shooting began. Hearing this, Che ordered his group to evacuate the village along a road leading to the Rio Grande. As they withdrew from La Higuera, those in the rear of the column came under heavy fire from the advancing troops. During the confusion, contact was lost with both Inti Peredo and the Bolivian called León. A short time later, Inti reached Che and the others, but León did not appear. With Inti reincorporated into the group, the guerrillas departed from the area by taking one of the ravines leading from the Rio Grande.

Understandably, the news of the encounter near La Higuera was received by the army high command and the Barrientos government as a clear sign that victory was almost within their grasp. Word was immediately sent to Vallegrande, where the new Ranger regiment Manchego No. 2 had just arrived after finishing nineteen weeks of special counterinsurgency training under the supervision of U.S. Army Special Forces personnel. By dawn on September 27, the first unit of this new regiment had already moved into the region around La Higuera. In fact, it was a unit of these American-trained Rangers that captured Camba (his real name was Orlando Jiménez Bazán) the day following the ambush. Camba's comrade, León, who deserted the guerrilla force on the day of the ambush, turned himself in to the authorities several days later.

In his diary, Che acknowledged that his losses were very great in the La Higuera encounter. He considered Coco the most grievous loss but noted that Miguel and Julio had been magnificent fighters and that the human value of all three was inexpressible. His diary also reveals that the last days of September were tense ones for him and his men. They were forced to move by night and hide during the day, and on more than one occasion they were nearly discovered by the soldiers.

By the end of the month, it was clear to everyone in Che's small force that they were in a desperate position. Not only was the circle of troops closing in around them, but their every movement was being reported to the army by the local population. Their plight was summed up by Che in his diary: "The characteristics are the same as last month, except now the army is demonstrating increasing effectiveness in its actions and the *campesinos* are giving us no support and have turned into informers.

"The most important task is to escape and look for more propitious zones; and then afterwards our contacts, in spite of the fact that the whole apparatus is disrupted in La Paz where they have given us severe blows." In view of the circumstances, however, Che and his comrades had little chance "to escape and look for more propitious zones." They were completely surrounded by thousands of troops and unable to move rapidly across the difficult terrain due to their wounds and fatigue.

CHAPTER 10

How Che Died

Throughout the first few days of October, Che and his men, now reduced to sixteen, spent most of the daylight hours on the crests of the ridges north of La Higuera and the nights in the hollows at the bases of these ridges. On the evening of October 3, Che heard a news broadcast concerning Camba and León, and Che made the following entry in his diary: "Both gave abundant information about Fernando [Che's own code name], his illness and everything else. . . . Thus ends the story of two heroic guerrillas." Che also commented sarcastically on a recorded interview which he had heard between a Bolivian student leader and imprisoned Regis Debray. The entry in his diary reads: "I heard an interview with Debray, very courageous in front of a student provocator." On October 4, Che wrote that he had heard a commentary on the radio whose conclusion had been that if he was captured by troops of the Fourth Army Division, he would be tried in Camiri, but if by the Eighth Division, he would be tried in Santa Cruz.

On Saturday, October 7, the last day for which there is an entry in Che's diary, he and his men camped in one of the many ravines near La Higuera. There they encounted an old woman herding goats and attempted to question her about the presence of soldiers in the area, but they were unable to obtain any reliable information. Afterwards, fearing that the old woman would report them, Che ordered two of his men to go to her house and pay her fifty pesos to keep quiet. He noted in his diary, however, that he had little hope that she would do as instructed. He began this last entry in his diary with a notation that it had been exactly eleven months since the inauguration of his guerrilla movement.

Apparently, the old woman or someone else who had seen Che and his group pass through the area reported their presence to the army post in La Higuera. By the morning of Sunday, October 8, several companies of Rangers were deployed in the zone through which Che's small force was moving. Early that morning Captain Gary Prado and his company of Rangers, all recent graduates of the U.S. Army Special Forces training camp near Santa Cruz, took up positions on the heights of the Quebrada de Yuro, one of the most rugged ravines in the area. Che and his men, after marching the night before, had stopped to rest in this ravine until they could resume marching under cover of darkness.

About noon, a unit from Prado's company made contact with the guerrillas. In this initial encounter, two soldiers were killed and several others wounded. Having located the guerrilla force, the lieutenant in charge of the small probing unit radioed Captain Prado for assistance. The subsequent series of events reads like a scenario out of a U.S. Army counterinsurgency manual. Captain Prado immediately deployed the rest of his troops in a circle around the guerrillas. Meanwhile, Che divided his small force into two groups in an effort to confuse the Rangers and escape. The group led by Che moved towards the closest exit from the ravine. However, the hill commanding this exit was occupied by a sizable number of troops and had been chosen by Captain Prado as the site of his command post. As Che and his group came within shooting range of Prado's men, they found themselves caught in a rain of automatic weapons fire.

Captain Prado watched the guerrillas disperse and run for cover through his field glasses and ordered Sergeant Bernardino Huanca and his men to descend in pursuit. A few minutes later, Sergeant Huanca fired a burst from his submachine gun at a guerrilla moving through a thicket of thorn bushes. One bullet sent the guerrilla's black beret flying off his head, while two others tore into his leg and forced him to the ground. The fallen guerrilla was Che. As he lay helpless the Rangers began to concentrate their fire on the area where he had fallen. But Willy (one of Moises Guevara's recruits, whom Che had begun to regard as a potential deserter) rushed to his side, and helped him out of the line of fire and up one side of the ravine. As the two scrambled upward, they ran into four Rangers who were positioning a mortar. The Rangers ordered them to surrender, but Che, supporting himself against a tree, fired his carbine in answer. The soldiers returned the fire. A few seconds later, a bullet hit the barrel of Che's carbine, rendering it useless and wounding him in the right forearm. At this point, Che reportedly raised his hands and shouted: "Stop! Don't shoot! I'm Che Guevara, and I'm worth more to you alive than dead." A few yards away, Willy threw down his rifle and also surrendered.

It was approximately 4:00 P.M. when Che and Willy were brought before Captain Prado. The latter immediately ordered his radio operator to signal the divisional headquarters in Vallegrande and tell them that Che Guevara had been captured. When the radio operator established contact with Vallegrande he shouted: "Hello, Saturno, we have Papa!" (Saturno was the code name for Colonel Joaquín Zenteno, commandant of the Eighth Bolivian Army Divison, and Papa was the code named used for Che.) In disbelief, Colonel Zenteno asked Captain Prado to confirm the message. Following the confirmation, there was general euphoria among the divisional headquarters staff. When the back-patting subsided, Colonel Zenteno radioed Prado to immediately transfer Che and any other prisoners to La Higuera.

Since the Rangers had come into the Quebrada de Yuro on foot, Che had to be transported the seven kilometers to La Higuera stretched out in a blanket carried by four soldiers. Willy was forced to walk behind with his hands tied against his back. They arrived in La Higuera shortly after dark. The prisoners were placed in the little town's two-room schoolhouse, Che in one room and Willy in the other. Later the Rangers brought in a third guerrilla, the Cuban Aniceto, who had been taken prisoner near where Che and Willy were captured. He was placed in the classroom with Willy. The bodies of four other guerrillas were also brought to La Higuera that night.

The remaining group of guerrillas, led by Inti Peredo, had gone to the opposite end of the Quebrada when Che ordered the column to separate. They were able to hold out until nightfall and then slip out of the ravine. In subsequent weeks, half the members of this second group were killed by the army. Of those who survived, the three remaining Cubans managed to flee the country, while Inti and the surviving Bolivians went into hiding.

During the night of October 8, and the next morning, Che was interrogated by a number of army officers, including Major Miguel Ayoroa, Colonel Andrés Selich, and Colonel Zenteno. He was also questioned by the CIA agent who called himself Dr. Eduardo Gonzales, one of the Cuban exiles sent by the CIA to participate in the counterinsurgency campaign against the guerrillas. Che refused to answer any of their questions, but he did talk to some of the officers and soldiers around him. At one point, one of the younger officers asked Che what he was thinking about. At first, Che ignored him, but when he overheard the officer say sarcastically to another officer that he (Che) was probably thinking about the immortality of the burro, Che answered: "No, I'm thinking about the immortality of the revolution!" On another occasion, one of the junior officers, who had drunk too much in celebration of Che's capture, tried to harass him. Che responded by punching the officer in the face. Although Che's wounds were painful, they were not serious, and he remained conscious during this entire period.

In La Paz, President Barrientos and the high command of the Bolivian Armed Forces held an emergency meeting to decide what to do with Che. They ruled out any prospect of prosecuting him through judicial proceedings, because a trial would focus world attention on him and present the Communists with a propaganda field day. Moreover, since Bolivia does not have the death penalty, they feared that if Che remained alive as their prisoner, sympathizers from all over the world would converge on Bolivia in an effort to save him or carry on his fight. They decided, therefore, that Che had to be executed immediately. However, officially it would be announced that he had died from wounds received in battle.

Early on the morning of Monday, October 9, the top-ranking officers in La Higuera received the order from La Paz to execute Che. They in turn instructed the noncommissioned officers present to carry out the order. Since none of the latter were anxious to do so, they chose lots to determine who would execute Che. Several hours before, these non-commissioned officers, as well as the soldiers on guard around the schoolhouse where Che was being held prisoner, had divided among themselves the money and personal objects taken from Che after his capture. His watch, compass, Parker fountain pen, two berets (including the one with a bullet hole through it), belt, stainless steel dagger, two pipes, and cigarette holder were the most important pieces of booty distributed among those who had had the honor of participating in the capture of the famous guerrilla leader.

Shortly before noon on Monday, some twenty-four hours after Che and his men had been discovered in the Quebrada de Yuro, Sergeant Jaime Terán walked to the little schoolhouse in La Higuera to carry out the order sent down from La Paz. He had drawn the shortest straw. When he entered the classroom where his victim was waiting, he found him propped up against one of the walls. Che guessed the nature of Sergeant Terán's mission and calmly asked to wait a moment until he stood up. Terán was so frightened by the prospect of what he had to do that he began to tremble. He turned and ran from the schoolhouse. But Colonel Selich and Colonel Zenteno ordered him to go back and shoot Che without further delay. Still trembling, Terán returned to the classroom, and without looking at his victim's face, he fired a burst from his carbine. The bullets slammed into Che's chest and side, passed through his body, and made large holes in the soft adobe wall of the classroom. The sergeant had been told not to inflect any wounds in Che's head or heart, so that the army could later claim that he had died from wounds received in combat. However, while Terán's carbine was still smoking, several soldiers pushed into the classroom. They said that they too wanted to shoot, so that they could boast that they had shot the famous Che Guevara. Sergeant Terán weakly nodded his approval and they began firing.

When the shooting was over, there were nine bullet wounds in Che's body, two of which were obviously instantaneously fatal. Moments later, Willy and Aniceto were executed by another sergeant in Captain Prado's company. The shooting resounded through the streets of the village, startling the townspeople and causing them to crowd around the little schoolhouse. In a short time, the entire town knew what had taken place there. For this reason, travel into the La Higuera area to this day remains strictly forbidden to outsiders. Moreover, the little schoolhouse has since been destroyed by the army, leaving no visible evidence of the shootings that took place there on October 9, 1967.

Soon after Che and his comrades were shot, the senior army officers and the CIA agent, Gonzales, left La Higuera by helicopter for the army headquarters in Vallegrande. Later in the afternoon, Che's body was wrapped in a canvas and strapped to the runner of a helicopter bound for Vallegrande. At the Vallegrande airstrip, nearly half the population of the town awaited the arrival of Che's body. Colonel Zenteno had announced several hours earlier that Che was dead and would soon be brought to Vallegrande.

When the helicopter arrived in Vallegrande, it landed on the side of the airstrip away from the crowd of townspeople, reporters, and soldiers. Before the rotor of the helicopter had stopped, Che's body was loaded into the back of a white Chevrolet panel truck (the type used as ambulances throughout most of Latin America) and transported at high speed through Vallegrande's narrow streets to the Señor de Malta Hospital.

The body was placed in an adobe shack apart from the main hospital building. In this shack several officials washed the blood from Che's body, made an incision in his neck for embalming fluid, and took his fingerprints. According to two British journalists who arrived on the scene early, the entire process appeared to be under the supervision of a CIA agent who fits the description given by others of Eduardo Gonzales. He refused to let the two journalists photograph Che, and when they asked him in English where he was from, he answered sarcastically, "From nowhere!"

Soon General Ovando, head of the Bolivian Armed Forces, and a number of other top military figures came to see the body of the famous guerrilla. By this time, a large crowd had excitedly collected around the shack. They probably would have broken through the cordon of soldiers trying to hold them back had it not been for the quick intervention of General Ovando. The general explained that they all had a right to see Che, but that they would have to wait until the officials had finished preparing and identifying the body.

Once the officials had finished their work, the soldiers allowed the waiting newsmen to enter the shack and take pictures. Afterwards, they let the townspeople file past to view the corpse. Throughout the night a silent file of staring townspeople, peasants, and soldiers passed by the body. Che's body was on a stretcher which had been placed across the length of a concrete laundry sink. He was nude from the waist up—the officials had removed his jacket during the preceding investigation and preparation—but the bullet wounds in his chest and sides were almost inconspicuous. He looked amazingly alive. Not only were his eyes open and brilliant, but there was a haunting smile on his lips. Pictures of this vibrant and serene expression were conveyed around the world by the news media.

Che's body was exhibited in the hospital at Vallegrande for approximately twenty-four hours. What happened to it afterwards is still a mystery. On October 11, General Ovando announced that the body had been buried in the Vallegrande area. The next day, however, General Ovando's office officially announced that the body had been incinerated, and President Barrientos said a few days later that Che's ashes had been buried in a hidden place somewhere in the Vallegrande region. Almost nine months later, an article in the Peruvian paper *La Prensa* claimed that members of

President Barrientos' personal guard had told a high functionary in the Peruvian police, when the Bolivian president visited Lima in July, that Che's body had been taken to the United States by the CIA in order to prevent it from falling into the hands of Marxists intent on sanctifying his remains. But a few days later, President Barrientos' personal guard publicly denied that any of its members had said anything to anyone about Che's body during the president's visit to Peru.

In any case, the rapid disposal of the body was probably motivated by the impending arrival in La Paz of Che's brother, Roberto Guevara, who was intent on claiming the body and taking it back to Argentina. When Roberto, a lawyer, arrived in Bolivia on October 12, he was told that it was impossible for him to see his brother's body since it had been cremated the day before. Not wanting to believe that his brother had been killed, Roberto asked to see the hands which the Bolivian officials claimed that they had cut from the body as proof that Che Guevara had been killed. But he was denied even this request and was forced to return to Argentina without having seen any evidence that his brother died in Bolivia. However, a few days later, a team of Argentine police experts arrived in La Paz in response to an invitation by President Barrientos. They were allowed to examine Che's hands and compare his fingerprints with those in the files of the Argentine Federal Police. On their departure, they issued an official statement to the effect that the fingerprints were identical and belonged to Ernesto "Che" Guevara.

The contradictions in the official statements given by the Bolivian authorities with regard to the disposition of Che's body were minor compared to those that appeared in statements concerning how and when Che died. On October 13, Dr. José Martínez, one of the two doctors at the Señor de Malta hospital who had been asked by the military to conduct an autopsy on Che's body, reported to the press that Che had received two mortal wounds, one in the lungs and the other in the heart. He also stated that on examining the body shortly after it had been brought to the hospital in Vallegrande, he had estimated that Che had died not more than five or six hours earlier. The doctor's statements obviously indicated that he had died from wounds he received shortly before being brought to Vallegrande, and *after* the battle in the Quebrada de Yuro. Yet on the same day as Dr. Martínez made his statement, Colonel Zenteno stated before a press conference that although he was not able to say precisely when Che had died, it was "almost immediately after he was wounded in combat." And on the same day, General Ovando stated that Che had died early Monday morning as a consequence of wounds received the previous afternoon in combat. Although Che could not have lived overnight with a fatal bullet wound in both his heart and lungs, General Ovando denied emphatically and indignantly the suggestion that Che had been shot to death after he was taken prisoner.

The seemingly endless capacity of the Bolivian officials to contradict themselves not only made it clear that Che had been executed, but also demonstrated that the government and military were incapable of accomplishing anything without creating confusion and making embarrassing errors. The government's bungling efforts at a later date to sell Che's campaign diary (obtained along with a number of other important items when he was captured in the Quebrada de Yuro), and the incredible circumstances surrounding the clandestine delivery of the diary to Cuba by none other than the top official in President Barrientos' cabinet, are further evidence of the weaknesses, both moral and otherwise, in the present regime. Indeed, the entire episode gives the appearance of a nightmarish comedy of errors.

CHAPTER 11

The Absence of Popular Support

The success of any guerrilla movement depends upon the degree of support it possesses among the civilian population in its area of operations. Che knew this fact and mentioned it frequently in his writings on guerrilla warfare. However, the complete absence of popular support for his guerrilla movement was one of the main reasons, if not the prime reason, that his operation in Bolivia failed.

Most professional military men mistakenly consider that the outcome of any guerrilla insurrection depends upon the military tactics used by the counter-guerrilla forces, the nature of the terrain in which the guerrillas operate, whether or not the guerrillas have a privileged sanctuary (such as the Viet Cong possess in Cambodia), and the extent of external assistance received by the guerrillas. In recent years, they have also begun to attach some importance to political measures designed to prevent the local population from supporting the guerrillas, but they tend to regard these as secondary in importance.

However, all the evidence indicates that military factors play a secondary role in determining the success or failure of revolutionary guerrilla insurrections. The crucial factor is clearly the degree of sympathy and support which the general population gives to the guerrillas. Widespread popular support has been the one characteristic universal to every successful guerrilla movement. In fact, it is only through the active assistance and cooperation of the general population that a guerrilla force can survive and go on to defeat the vastly superior forces of the regime it opposes.

Revolutionary guerrilla warfare depends upon, and is a struggle for, the loyalties of the civilian population. Close guerrilla-civilian cooperation enables the guerrillas to develop a superior system of intelligence, extreme mobility, an inexhaustable source of supplies, and the ability to surprise the enemy's forces when they are off-guard. Without close ties to the civilian population, they cannot develop even this minimal level of capabilities vital to successful guerrilla warfare.

For example, in the area of intelligence, which is both a military necessity and a major factor contributing to the morale of the guerrillas, the cooperation of the civilian population is of paramount importance. The guerrillas are dependent upon the local population for the information they need in order to know the location of the enemy's forces, to discover his points of weakness, and to escape his efforts to trap them. In order to obtain this kind of information on a systematic and continuing basis, the guerrillas must organize a widespread civilian intelligence network. This kind of a civilian spy system gives the guerrillas a great advantage over the enemy's forces, since every movement they make takes place within a "fishbowl." This intelligence capability, plus the citizenry's provision of food, supplies, and shelter to the guerrillas, also give the guerrillas greater mobility than the enemy troops. With the entire population as their logistics and intelligence system, they are able to operate with far greater independence than the enemy's regular forces.

Past instances of guerrilla-led insurrections indicate that a guerrilla movement can obtain widespread popular support only if the general population feels a strong sense of hostility toward the existing political authorities. In this kind of situation, the guerrillas can win the support of the general population by virtue of the fact that they are fighting against the "enemies of the people." In other words, the population supports the guerrillas not because of their identification with the guerrillas' long-range political objectives or ideological doctrine, but because the guerrillas are intent upon removing the existing authorities from power and thereby eliminating the main cause of the local population's grievances.

One of the reasons Che's guerrilla movement failed to obtain any popular support in Bolivia is that the majority of Bolivians believe their country has already undergone its revolution of national liberation. Although Che visited Bolivia shortly after the revolution of 1952, he failed to perceive either then or later how much importance the Bolivians attach to this event. In fact, for many Bolivians, the revolution of 1952 is regarded in much the same way as the Cubans regard their recent revolution. Because Che did not understand this fact, and because his Bolivian sources of information did not convey it to him, he believed his guerrilla movement would be able to capitalize on the hostility and discontent which he assumed the Bolivian people felt toward their political leaders.

What Che failed to understand is that the revolution of 1952 gave the Bolivian masses, for the first time in Bolivian history, a real stake in the social order as well as a sense of involvement in the larger political and cultural community. Despite the military coup of 1964 and the consequent fall from power of the National Revolutionary Movement (the group which spearheaded the revolution of 1952 and ruled the country until the coup), the changes set in motion by the revolution continue to have relevance for most of the Bolivian population today.

The revolution of 1952 was neither a barracks revolt nor a middle-class rebellion; it was a true popular revolution based upon a new sense of Bolivian nationalism. Its goal was nothing less than the dismemberment of the old social, economic, and political order. Consequently, one of the first things the new revolutionary government did was to nationalize the country's three largest tin mines. Since tin is the basis of Bolivia's national economy, the nationalization of these mines was an act of tremendous symbolic importance. On the basis of this act alone, the new government was able to claim that control over the country's national wealth had been taken away from the hands of special interests and given to the Bolivian people.

As a result of the revolution of 1952, new legislation was passed which gave to all of Bolivia's adult citizens, whether literate or not, the right to vote. Previous literacy requirements had limited the vote to the country's large landholders and to the middle and upper classes in the cities. The new electoral law enfranchised for the first time Bolivia's rural masses, miners, and urban working class. Thus, for the first time in the history of the country, these groups were given true citizenship and a voice in the national political process.

The revolution of 1952 also brought about extensive land reform. However, it was not so much the new revolutionary government as the peasants themselves who organized and carried out the dismemberment of the former feudal estates and the redistribution of their lands. The role played by the new government was simply to provide the machinery for formalizing the redistribution of land which had already been carried out by the peasants. The latter, organized into local "agragrian syndicates," declared war on the large landowners shortly after the revolution began in La Paz. They killed or chased away their former landlords, expropriated their lands, and confiscated their houses, vehicles, and farm equipment. Thus, it was the peasants themselves who were responsible for the land reform measures associated with the revolution of 1952, and the sense of self-esteem which possession of their own land has given them continues to be one of the most significant consequences of the revolution.

The revolution of 1952 liquidated Bolivia's landed aristocracy and produced a newly awakened and politically mobilized peasantry. The agrarian syndicates formed to acquire land for the peasants have since become important political organizations. In the Cochabamba Valley alone, these syndicates are capable of mobilizing over five hundred thousand armed men on relatively short notice. As a result, they are an important source of political power in Bolivia today. In fact, armed peasant militias have put down uprisings in Santa Cruz and miners' strikes on the *altiplano*. Moreover, for the first time in Bolivian history, peasants have been elected to the national legislature and appointed to such local political posts as mayor and sub-prefect. These developments have had a profound impact on the character of Bolivian politics and have contributed greatly to the growing sense of national consciousness among Bolivia's rural masses.

Che failed to see all of this and was misled into thinking that the peasantry and the workers would provide a popular base for his revolutionary guerrilla movement. However, the conditions for creating a successful revolutionary *foco* were obviously not present in Bolivia. In the first place, the guerrillas could not win the support of the rural masses by offering to give them land. Since 1952, Bolivia's peasants have controlled the land and the entire countryside. Moreover, they have seen some improvement in their social and economic status and they have hopes of greater improvement. This is not to say that they are well off, for their present situation is still one of the worst in Latin America. Nevertheless, they are much better off than they were in the past. Furthermore, the peasants are not isolated from the centers of national political power. Through their local syndicates they have a significant voice in the country's political affairs, and certain groups, such as the *campesinos* in the Cochabamba area, even have direct access to the president. Consequently, they do not regard the present political authorities as enemies of the people.

In view of the peasantry's increased involvement in national affairs, they perceived Che's guerrilla movement in totally different terms than he expected. Instead of supporting the guerrilla movement they opposed it. For example, at the end of June, 1967, the National Congress of Farm Workers issued a public declaration in which they denounced the guerrillas as an "anti-national force, financed from abroad and destined to create nothing but confusion and disruption." This group further stated that they were ready to cooperate with the armed forces "in totally liquidating this foreign aggression that is attempting to undermine in a systematic manner the economic and social development of our people."

The fact that the Bolivian public perceived the guerrillas as foreigners seriously handicapped the guerrilla movement. Saddled with this stigma, it was impossible for them to win widespread popular support among the general population. In fact, certain Bolivian observers have referred to the foreign character of Che's guerrilla movement as its "original sin." Since the guerrilla operation was neither organized nor led by Bolivians, it aroused the nationalistic emotions of nearly every segment of Bolivian society. The foreign character of the guerrilla operation also made it possible for President Barrientos to wrap himself in the Bolivian flag and play the role of defender of the Bolivian nation.

Che failed to note that the Barrientos regime was not a typical right-wing military government. First of all, Barrientos was popularly elected to the presidency in 1966. Afterwards, he attempted to build a broad base of popular support for his regime by courting the peasant syndicates. In addition, he cloaked his regime in many of the legitimizing symbols of the revolution of 1952 and promised to extend the social and economic reform measures put into practice since the revolution. Furthermore, to a degree unparalleled in Bolivian history, Barrientos traveled from one end of the country to the other to meet with the general public and talk to local political leaders. His showmanship and his command of both Aymará and Quechua (the two major Indian languages in Bolivia) earned him the respect and support of a large proportion of the population. At times, Barrientos displayed a remarkable degree of flexibility. For example, he appointed four Marxist politicians to his cabinet during the height of the guerrillas' activities. In his reply to the confusion and criticism which followed this move, he indicated that he was not opposed to Marxists per se, so long as they operated within the democratic process and did not engage in illegal activities against the state.

In view of these facts, Che's efforts to establish a revolutionary guerrilla *foco* in Bolivia appear to have been in violation of one of the fundamental precepts of his own theory of revolutionary guerrilla warfare. In his writings on guerrilla warfare, Che made it clear that it is impossible for a guerrilla movement to succeed in a country where the government (1) has risen to power by some form of popular consultation, (2) maintains at least the appearance of constitutional legality, and (3) gives the people some hope that their social and economic status will be improved.

In his introduction to the Cuban edition of Che's diary, Fidel Castro claims that the unresponsiveness of the Bolivian peasantry did not surprise Che. Castro claims that Che knew their mentality perfectly and that he therefore knew that it would require prolonged and patient work to win them over to the cause for which he and his men were fighting. However, it is difficult to accept Fidel's assertion in this regard when one takes into consideration the fact that Che's diary is filled with bitter remarks about the indifference and suspicion that he and his men encountered in their contacts with the local peasantry.

In the months following the outbreak of hostilities, Che became increasingly preoccupied with his movement's lack of support among the peasantry. He wrote: "The inhabitants of the region are as impenetrable as rocks. You speak to them, but in the depths of their eyes you can see that they do not believe you." Not only did the peasants distrust the guerrillas, but they also gave information to the authorities about their movements. On the same day that the Anglo-Chilean reporter George Roth encountered the guerrillas, Che discovered that two peasants from whom they had bought food a few days earlier had given information to the authorities. It seems that they were motivated to do so by the government's offer of a five-hundred-dollar reward to anyone providing information that would lead to the capture of the guerrillas.

Throughout the first month after the outbreak of hostilities, the guerrillas found that the vast majority of the local peasantry were both frightened and suspicious of them. In his monthly summary at the end of April, Che wrote that they had as yet failed to build a base of peasant support, but through "planned terror" he felt they could "neutralize" the peasants and gain their support later. This is surprising, in view of Che's previous opposition to the use of terrorism as a tactic of revolutionary guerrilla warfare, and probably reflects the extent of Che's frustration with the local peasantry's attitude toward his guerrilla movement. At any rate, neither he nor his men subsequently committed any acts that could be considered as terrorism against the peasant population. Apart from detaining as temporary prisoners *campesinos* whom they feared would give their presence away to government troops close at hand, the guerrillas treated the local peasantry with kid gloves.

During the month of May, 1967, Che's group encountered a few peasants who, in their desire to get rid of the guerrillas and avoid any trouble, sold them food and information (mostly about the location of watering places and roads). Consequently, at the end of the month, Che wrote in his diary that there was still a complete absence of peasant support for the movement, but that it appeared that his group was gradually winning the admiration of the peasants and dispelling their fears. He also mentioned that the army had issued an order for the detention of all those who collaborated with his force. He expressed the hope that this marked the beginning of a period in which both sides would exert pressure on the peasants. He made it clear that he anticipated that the army would use methods that would alienate the peasants and turn them toward the guerrillas.

By the end of June, Che was forced to admit that instead of alienating the local peasantry, the army was successfully turning them against the guerrilla movement. He wrote in his diary that even though the army continued to be ineffective in the military sphere, they were working on the peasants in a manner that could not be underestimated. In fact, he noted that through the clever use of fear and deceit the army was convincing the entire rural population to act as informers against his guerrilla force. These observations were based upon his discovery that the army had been working on the peasants in even the most isolated parts of the area in which the guerrillas were operating. In addition, he had discovered that many of the peasants in the area belonged to a *campesino* syndicate that supported the Barrientos government. Probably as a result of his recognition of the unfavorable prospects for obtaining popular support in the local area, Che noted that his group was caught in a vicious circle: in order to obtain peasant support they needed to carry out permanent action in a populated area, but in order to do this they needed to recruit more men, and this was impossible in view of their lack of popular support. Between the time that the guerrillas were discovered by the army in March and their defeat some six months later, they were not able to recruit a single person.

Throughout July, August, and September, the guerrillas tried to win the peasantry's confidence by offering them very high prices for food and other items. But this did not allay the fears of the peasants, who did almost everything they could to avoid the guerrillas. For example, on July 7, Che wrote in his diary that a peasant from whom they had bought a pig that day had warned them that there were some two hundred soldiers nearby. But the next day Che learned that there were no soldiers in the immediate area and that the peasant had lied to them in order to make them leave his farm. By the end of September, the situation was far more serious, and Che was forced to acknowledge that not only were they not making any gains with the peasantry, but that, in fact, the majority of the peasants had turned to informing on them. Indeed, it was a local peasant who gave the Rangers the information which led to Che's capture.

In view of the alien character of the guerrillas it is not difficult to understand why the local peasantry reacted negatively toward them. But it *is* difficult to understand how Che could have overlooked this problem. Regis Debray certainly seems to have been aware of it. In both his 1965 article, "Castroism: The Long March in Latin America," and his book, *Revolution in the Revolution?*, Debray calls attention to the parochialism and distrust of strangers that characterize the population in the rural areas of Latin America. According to Debray, the mentality of the peasants in these areas makes it extremely difficult for a guerrilla force to win their support and cooperation. Past experience has taught them to distrust the outsider, the white man, and the stranger. For this reason, Debray says, the guerrillas, and not the government troops, are most likely to be regarded by the local peasantry as the foreigners. Apart from their being strangers without any status in the local area, their presence in the area generates the unpleasant prospect of government repression, bloodshed, and the destruction of property.

Even if Che's group had not been marked with the stigma of "foreign intruders," it seems highly unlikely they would have been able to establish a base of popular support among the peasantry in the southeast of Bolivia. The fact that they *were* considered foreigners, of course, made it impossible for them to develop any popular support among the local peasantry, and so they found themselves isolated and surrounded on all sides by informers and government sympathizers.

CHAPTER 12

The Communist Betrayal and Leftist Abandonment of the Guerrillas

⌐⌐⌐⌐⌐⌐⌐⌐⌐⌐⌐⌐⌐⌐⌐⌐⌐⌐⌐⌐⌐⌐⌐⌐

In what is now a familiar pattern throughout most of the developing states of Latin America, Asia, and Africa, Bolivia's Marxists are deeply divided among a number of separate and opposing political groups. Due to the conflict between the Soviet Union and Red China, Bolivia's Communists are split into two hostile political factions: the Bolivian Communist Party (pro-Moscow) and the New Bolivian Communist Party (pro-Peking). Each claims the other has betrayed the Marxist-Leninist cause. The pro-Peking Communists refer to the pro-Moscow Communists as "revisionists," perhaps the dirtiest word in the Communist lexicon, and speak of themselves as true Marxist-Leninists. The pro-Moscow Communists, on the other hand, pretend their party is the only Communist party in Bolivia, but when forced to speak of the pro-

Peking group, they refer to them contemptuously as *Maoistas* or *Pekinistas*.

However, the majority of Bolivia's Marxists are not members of either of these two Communist groups. They are dispersed among a variety of left-wing political parties, the most important of these being the Trotskyite Workers' Revolutionary Party (which is divided into two factions), the Revolutionary Party of the Nationalist Left, the Party of the Revolutionary Left, and the National Revolutionary Movement. Due to their ideological differences and competition for public support, there is little love lost between the Marxists in this bewildering array of left-wing political parties.

Che's efforts to obtain political support for his guerrilla operation were decisively influenced by the fragmentation of Bolivia's Marxists as well as by the conflict which exists between the Soviet Union, Red China, and Cuba over who shall control the Communist movement in Latin America. With regard to the latter, it is important to note that the Cuban Communists like to think of themselves as a third force, as an alternative to the pro-Moscow and pro-Peking Communists in Latin America. They advocate the Castro-Guevara doctrine of promoting socialist revolutions in Latin America through the creation of revolutionary guerrilla movements based on the Cuban model. They also argue that the Cuban Revolution has demonstrated that an insurrectionary guerrilla force can be an effective substitute for the Communist Party, taking the Party's place as the revolutionary vanguard of the masses. They argue that the guerrillas, instead of the Party, are best able to mobilize the masses and lead them in an armed struggle to gain power. Only after power has been seized do they concede that a Marxist-Leninist party is a necessary condition for the establishment of a socialist society.

Castro has stated that he is willing to work with all those who want to join the revolutionary struggle against imperialism in Latin America. For example, in March, 1967, he publically stated that Cuba would give its total support to those political parties in Latin America which consistently take a revolutionary position. He also said that in any country where the Communists do not show themselves disposed to carry out their revolutionary duties, Cuba would support those who are *true* revolutionaries. In sum, the Castroites claim that the revolution comes first and ideological concerns second, and that in any given country of Latin America a revolutionary guerrilla force can unite all the anti-imperialist and revolutionary groups within the country, whatever their political label.

Both the pro-Moscow and pro-Peking Communists find it impossible to accept the doctrine that the Communist Party can be replaced in the Latin American setting by a revolutionary guerrilla movement. They firmly believe that their respective parties must be the sole source of leadership and ideological direction for any Marxist revolutionary undertaking. Moreover, they cannot accept the Castroite assumption that it is possible for revolutionaries holding different ideological positions to work together.

Of the two groups, the pro-Peking Communists have more in common with the Castroites than the pro-Moscow Communists, since the *Pekinistas* agree that an armed revolution is the only way to liberate the masses of Latin America from imperialist exploitation and domestic oppression. However, the pro-Peking Communists believe that they must first educate the masses in order to make them politically conscious of their oppressed and exploited condition, whereas the Castroites argue that it is not possible to awaken the revolutionary consciousness of the predominantly rural and illiterate masses of Latin America without first initiating insurrectionary focal points throughout the continent. The pro-Peking Communists also firmly believe that the revolution requires "correct" Marxist-Leninist planning and direction if it is to succeed. They contend, therefore, that it cannot be entrusted to those who do not have a clear Marxist-Leninist (i.e., pro-Peking) ideological orientation.

In Bolivia, the pro-Peking position has been defined by Oscar Zamora, leader of the New Bolivian Communist Party. He has made it quite clear on a number of occasions that his party believes the Bolivian people can only be liberated by a revolutionary force whose leadership is Marxist-Leninist (pro-Peking), and free of all counterrevolutionary currents, particularly "contemporary revisionism" (i.e., pro-Moscow Communism). Moreover, Zamora has stressed that the political mobilization of the masses, especially the workers and peasants, is inseparable from any armed struggle, and that this political activity must be carried out before and during the armed struggle by his party.

In contrast, the pro-Moscow Communists in Bolivia argue that a guerrilla-led insurrection is only one of the many forms of struggle that the masses and their political vanguard, the Communist Party, can adopt in their fight to wrest power from the imperialists and their lackeys. In line with their instructions from Moscow, the pro-Moscow Communists in Bolivia and throughout Latin America are attempting to pursue a policy of peaceful coexistence with the present regimes. Consequently, they have restricted most of their efforts to gain power to legal and parliamentary means. Moscow's reasoning is that there is little likelihood that the U.S. will allow another Cuban-type revolution to succeed anywhere in Latin America. Therefore, her current strategy involves offering the Latin American countries generous economic aid while at the same time assisting the pro-Moscow Communist parties in these countries in their new efforts to win popular support through more or less legitimate means.

However, the pro-Moscow Communists in Latin America realize that by following this policy of peaceful coexistence they risk losing much of their support to more revolutionary groups, such as the pro-Peking Communists and the Castroites, who advocate the immediate change of the existing order through the use of force. Consequently, the pro-Moscow Communists pay lip-service to the idea of an armed revolution when they are in leftist circles. But they say that the right moment has not arrived to launch the revolution. Until this moment arrives, they claim their party must follow a policy which will allow it to operate openly among the masses.

Castro's independent brand of revolutionary Marxism, and particularly Che's attempts to put it into practice, have seriously threatened the position of pro-Moscow Communists in Latin

America. It is extremely difficult for them to control their more militant members and pursue their policy of "struggle within legality" with individuals like Che Guevara calling for the immediate establishment of revolutionary guerrilla *focos* throughout Latin America.

After the division of the Bolivian Communist Party into two opposing political groups in early 1965, Castro, under pressure from Moscow, refused to recognize the pro-Peking group and thereafter confined his relations to the pro-Moscow Communists. Thus, only the pro-Moscow group was invited to send a delegation to the Tricontinental Conference held in Havana in January, 1966. Much to the surprise of the Cubans, however, these pro-Moscow delegates from Bolivia took a position at the conference which was far more revolutionary than would have been expected from loyal supporters of the Moscow line. Apparently, the Bolivian delegates outdid themselves in paying lip-service to armed revolution. This was undoubtedly because the position taken by most of the other delegates to the conference was quite revolutionary and they did not want to appear less militant than the others.

The Bolivian delegation did such a good job of acting like zealous revolutionaries that they gave the Cubans the impression that they might be interested in establishing a revolutionary guerrilla *foco* in Bolivia. Consequently, Castro arranged a secret meeting with the Bolivian delegation to discuss the possibility of such an undertaking. The Bolivians were quite surprised when they discovered that Castro wanted to give them large sums of money to organize a guerrilla operation in Bolivia. Their commitment to the Moscow line obligated them to refrain from engaging in any overt revolutionary action such as guerrilla warfare. However, according to reliable informants in Bolivia, the prospect of swindling the Cubans out of large sums of money led the leader of the Bolivian delegation, Mario Monje, to pretend that his party was interested in organizing a guerrilla operation in Bolivia if the Cubans would give them the necessary financial support. To bait the Cubans, Monje told Castro that the political situation in Bolivia was ripe for a Cuban-type revolution, and that his party had widespread support among the peasantry and workers.

Monje's exaggerated description of conditions in Bolivia and of his party's popular support convinced Castro that Bolivia was an ideal country for a revolutionary guerrilla *foco*. As a result, he promised Monje considerable Cuban support if he would organize a guerrilla force there. At this point, of course, there was no mention of Che's going to Bolivia, since he was still in the Congo at that time. Castro did offer, however, to send a contingent of Cubans to Bolivia to help Monje and his comrades train their guerrilla force. As might be expected, Monje reacted quite negatively to this suggestion, insisting that any guerrilla operation in his country would have to be completely Bolivian in composition. Although Castro disagreed with Monje on this point, he did not press the matter at the time. Consequently, Monje came away from the meeting believing he had Castro's promise of financial support for his fraudulent scheme.

Following the Tricontinental Conference, Castro requested additional information from Monje on conditions in Bolivia, and Monje continued to portray his country as an ideal place to launch a guerrilla-led revolution. Therefore, when Che returned to Havana from the Congo and spoke with Castro about his desire to direct a guerrilla operation in South America, Castro suggested that he consider Bolivia as the base for his operation. This, plus the considerations discussed earlier, led Che to choose Bolivia as the center for his first guerrilla *foco*.

The only major drawback with regard to Bolivia was that Monje had previously insisted that any future revolutionary struggle in Bolivia would have to be solely Bolivian in composition and under the direct control of his party. Furthermore, Che had been informed by his own contacts in Bolivia that Monje and his group had a habit of working against any Communists who did not adhere to the Moscow line. Nevertheless, Che discounted these considerations and decided to take a hand-picked contingent of Cubans to Bolivia and establish the initial base for his revolutionary movement there.

Because of Cuba's relationship with the Soviet Union, Castro asked Che not to deal with the pro-Peking group in Bolivia and to try and obtain the cooperation of Monje and his party once Che was in Bolivia. However, it seems clear that Che never really expected that Monje's party would openly join forces with him. Nor did this consideration discourage him, for his intention was to establish a force devoid of any sectarian spirit, one which would incorporate all those who were willing to fight for the liberation not only of Bolivia but of Latin America as a whole.

The primary preparations for the guerrilla operation in Bolivia were entrusted to a small number of Castroite sympathizers within Monje's party. But these individuals, whom Castro calls "valuable and discreet collaborators" in his introduction to the Cuban edition of Che's diary, worked secretly for Che without informing anyone, including Monje and their other party leaders, about what they were doing. As a result, Monje was not informed of Che's guerrilla operation until after Che arrived in Bolivia. As can be imagined, the news came as quite a shock to Monje, particularly since he had been under the impression that Castro was going to provide *him* with financial support to organize a guerrilla force in Bolivia.

It was in mid-December that Monje was informed by Havana that Che was in the southeast of Bolivia and that he wanted to meet with Monje to discuss the launching of a guerrilla force in that area. Shocked that Che was in the country and uncertain as to what his plans were, Monje agreed to meet Che at his camp in the Ñancahuazú area. At this point, Monje had no idea that Che planned to stay in Bolivia and that he wanted to launch an armed struggle destined to encompass all of Latin America. Consequently, Monje went to the Ñancahuazú meeting with the idea that he might still be able to gain Cuban support for an operation which, under his control, would never develop into anything but an expansion of his party's treasury. Certainly, Monje had no intention of involving his party, against Moscow's orders, in an armed struggle against the Barrientos regime.

Monje arrived at Che's camp on New Year's Eve. The entry in

Che's diary for that date indicates that Monje's reception was cordial but tense. Che noted that the question "Why are you here?" hung in the atmosphere, revealing that when Monje arrived he was still unsure about why Che was in Bolivia. This entry in Che's diary, as well as that recorded for the same day in the diary of one of the other guerrillas, reveals that in response to Che's request for his party's support, Monje made it clear that his party could not officially support the guerrilla operation. However, he offered to resign from the party, obtain at least its neutrality, and bring several cadres of men to join those already in training, provided Che agreed to give him both the political and military command of the entire operation, and a free hand to seek the support of the Communist parties in the other South American countries where Che planned to extend his guerrilla movement.

Monje's conditions for supporting the guerrilla movement were totally unacceptable to Che. He told Monje that he could accept no conditions concerning his leadership of the military operations. He knew that in the kind of revolutionary struggle he was planning, the military leadership of the struggle would have to come from the guerrilla force itself, not from a politician or group of politicians hundreds of miles from the scene of battle. Nor was he about to turn over the command of a movement which, in its final phase, would engulf all of Latin America to a man who lacked both the proper revolutionary vision as well as the necessary military experience. As for Monje's resigning from his position as leader of the Party, Che said that he considered this a tremendous error, since it would accommodate those (his party) who should be publically condemned for their hypocrisy.

Having reached a deadlock in the discussion, Monje told Che he wanted some time to think over the whole matter and asked if he could talk to the Bolivian members of Che's group. Che agreed and took Monje to the area nearby where most of the group were bivouacked. Monje met with the Bolivians and told them that they could stay with Che and be expelled from the Party, or support the Party and return with him to La Paz. Much to Monje's surprise, all the Bolivians present said they preferred to stay with Che.

The next morning, Monje announced that he was leaving for La Paz. He claimed that as soon as he returned he was going to resign his position in the Party and retire. Che noted in his diary that Monje left looking as though he were being led to the gallows. Actually, this was all a rather transparent deception on the part of Monje, since it is clear he never had any intention of resigning from his post as Party leader. Che appears to have seen through Monje's subterfuge at the time. He noted in his diary that after Monje discovered from Coco that he (Che) would not compromise on the crucial question of who was to lead the movement, Monje obstinately persisted in his demand for the number one post. Che realized that Monje had disagreed with him over who should command the movement as a pretext to escape any responsibility for working with the guerrillas.

If Monje had accepted the political leadership of the movement (while deferring to Che's military leadership) and had sent members of his party to fight with Che's nuclear group, then the guerrilla operation might not have suffered from the stigma of being directed and organized by foreigners. As it was, the Bolivian government was able to argue convincingly once hostilities began that the guerrillas were foreigners intervening in the domestic affairs of the country.

When Monje learned from Che that he was planning to organize and direct a guerrilla movement designed to turn all of Latin America into another Vietnam, he knew he had no choice but to disassociate himself from the undertaking. First of all, he regarded the operation as totally impractical. Secondly, he was not willing to break with Moscow and submit to the Castroite line. Finally, for Monje to have involved himself in a guerrilla operation would have been counter to his own personal interests. As leader of the pro-Moscow group, he enjoyed a comfortable bureaucratic life in La Paz. Joining Che and his guerrillas would have meant giving this up for a life of hardship and danger. This was a sacrifice which it appears Monje would not have been willing to make under even the most favorable circumstances.

When Monje returned to La Paz, he called an emergency meeting of his party's central committee. He told them of Che's presence in the country and of his plans to initiate a guerrilla movement which would extend into other neighboring countries. It was agreed that Che had presented the party with a very grave problem. If they supported him they would be acting contrary to Moscow's Latin American strategy and jeopardizing the very survival of their own party. Moreover, they all agreed that there was little chance the operation would succeed. On the other hand, if they didn't support Che, there was the possibility he might actually succeed in overthrowing the existing regime with the help of the pro-Peking group, or even worse, the Trotskyites. Nevertheless, it was decided that the party could not afford to take the risk of co-operating with the guerrillas.

Following this meeting, Monje sent a letter to Castro criticizing him for not having respected his position that any guerrilla operation in Bolivia would have to be totally Bolivian in composition. He told Castro that since the guerrilla force was largely Cuban in composition and Che was its leader, it was doomed to failure. He wrote this letter not because he wanted the leadership of the guerrilla movement for himself, but because he wanted to justify his refusal to collaborate with the guerrillas.

After Monje left, Che called all the members of his group together and explained to them what had transpired in his talks with the Communist leader. He told them that the Party had refused to support the guerrilla operation, and that, as a result, they were now free to unite with all those who wanted to bring about the revolution. He expressed the belief that while Monje's attitude might detrimentally affect the guerrilla movement in the short run, it would contribute to its development in the long run by freeing it of any political entanglements.

If Che felt this way, why then had he asked Monje for his support in the first place? The answer is to be found in Castro's intro-

duction to Che's diary. There Castro states that it was in defer-
ence to his Bolivian comrades who were members of the pro-Moscow party that Che made an effort to gain Monje's support, even
though he distrusted Monje. Che also noted in his diary that one
of the Bolivian members of his group, Bigotes, was willing to collaborate with him whatever the Party did, but also respected
Monje and seemed to care for him. Like Bigotes, most of Che's
Bolivian comrades were members of Monje's party, and they were
reluctant to fight for a cause which did not have the backing of
their party. In view of this, Che's effort to secure Monje's support
is understandable.

It is quite clear, however, that Che never expected the pro-Moscow Communists in Bolivia to support his guerrilla operation. For
example, on December 12, several weeks before his meeting with
Monje, Che gave his group a lecture on the realities of war and
warned the Bolivians in the group of the responsibility they had
undertaken by adopting "another line and violating party discipline." This indicates that Che had recruited the Bolivian members
of his force with the expectation that the pro-Moscow party would
most likely not approve of their participation in it. In reality, Che
hoped to steal the most militant and revolutionary members of
Monje's party and, with recruits from other groups, to build a
non-sectarian revolutionary force.

At the end of January, 1967, Che made a reference in his diary
to his meeting on New Year's Eve with Monje. He wrote that, as
he had expected, Monje's attitude had been at first evasive and
later traitorous. He also noted that "the Party was taking up arms
against his group" and that he didn't know where it all would
lead. However, he seems to have viewed these developments from
a very optimistic perspective, for he wrote that he was almost certain the Party's actions would prove to be beneficial to his cause in
the long run.

It is hard to imagine how Che could have believed that the opposition of the pro-Moscow group would prove to be beneficial to
his guerrilla movement. His reluctance to be tied to the pro-Moscow Communists is understandable, but it is difficult to see how

he could have failed to realize that their open opposition to his cause would not only deny him the manpower and urban support that he vitally needed but also lead to efforts on their part to sabotage his entire operation. Perhaps Che assumed that they would not dare attempt to sabotage an undertaking which was under his personal leadership and which had Castro's backing.

Following his meeting with Monje, Che notified Castro that Monje had refused to support the guerrilla operation and that Monje's party appeared to be opposed to the undertaking. Castro then contacted Jorge Kolle, number two man in the pro-Moscow party, and Simón Reyes, the pro-Moscow trade union leader, and asked them to come to Havana to discuss the guerrilla operation. They arrived in Havana during the first part of February, and, according to the message which Che received from Castro, the latter was quite hard on both of these Communist leaders. But Kolle gave Castro the excuse that he had not been aware of the intended continental magnitude of the guerrilla movement, which of course was a lie. He also told Castro that as soon as he returned to Bolivia he would go to see Che in order to discuss with him how the Party could help the guerrilla operation.

Kolle returned to Bolivia in mid-February, and although he stated several times over the next four or five months that he supported the guerrillas and was going to the southeast to visit Che, neither his trip to the guerrilla camp nor his promised support ever materialized. In fact, in the March 25 entry in his diary, Che contrasted Kolle's announced intention to come and discuss how he could help the guerrillas with his party's simultaneous expulsion of all the Bolivian members of his force from the youth wing of the Party.

Following the army's discovery of the guerrillas in March, 1967, and the publicity that ensued, the pro-Moscow leaders stated publicly that they supported the guerrillas. The leadership felt that it was necessary to make it appear that they supported the guerrilla operation in order to pacify their party's middle-level leaders and militants who were in sympathy with the guerrillas. As it was, they cleverly deceived their members into believing that the Party was giving the guerrillas full support, and that the relations of the leadership with Che were of the most cordial kind. In addition, Monje and Kolle were able to prevent the more militant members from going to join the guerrillas by convincing them that the guerrillas had no need for their services. Thus, while the pro-Moscow leaders were making declarations of support for the guerrillas, they were preventing their people from going to join the guerrillas and doing everything they could to sabotage the movement's chances of success.

In May, 1967, when Che's group was totally isolated from contact with either Havana or La Paz, an editorial in the pro-Moscow party newspaper *Unidad* stated that the Party's position was one of "support and solidarity with the guerrilla struggle" and that this support would be in the areas of organization, logistics, information, and propaganda, in order "to prevent the isolation" of the guerrilla force. The editorial conspicuously avoided any mention of sending contingents to join the guerrillas, and it is clear that the party leadership had no intention of assisting the guerrillas even in the areas of organization, logistics, information, and propaganda. Indeed, it was largely because of the pro-Moscow leaders that Che and his group were isolated at the very time this editorial was written. Ironically, the same editorial went on to state that, above all else, the guerrilla movement needed to be supported by the effective work of the Party among the masses. The fact is that the party leadership knew full well that the guerrillas had little chance of obtaining the support of the masses, since they had no intention of using the Party apparatus to mobilize popular support in favor of the guerrillas.

When the middle-level leaders and militants of the pro-Moscow party finally realized that their top leaders had not provided the guerrillas with the support that they claimed they were giving them, many of them demanded that they be allowed to go to the southeast and fight with Che. However, by this time it was too late. Che and his battered little group were completely surrounded, and the party leadership was able to argue in a convincing manner that the guerrillas were beyond help.

In spite of the fact that the Party did absolutely nothing to help Che, they didn't hesitate to take credit for supporting the guerrilla operation in left-wing circles. An example of this occurred at the July, 1967, inaugural meeting of the Latin American Organization of Solidarity, the Latin American regional subsidiary of the Tricontinental. At the start of the deliberations, held in Havana, Che was proclaimed president *in absentia* of the meeting by the delegates as a sign of their support for his revolutionary ideals. The Bolivian delegation, which was composed exclusively of representatives from the pro-Moscow Bolivian Communist Party, tried to give all those present the impression that they were working hand in hand with the guerrillas fighting in the southeast of Bolivia. In fact, on August 3, one of the Bolivian delegates went so far as to read a message to the meeting which was supposedly from the guerrillas. On hearing of this later, Che sarcastically noted in his diary that the message must have been the result of "telepathy." Elsewhere, he wrote that the meeting appeared to have been a triumph, but that "the Bolivian delegation was a pile of shit."

In his introduction to Che's diary, Castro bluntly accuses Mario Monje of having sabotaged Che's guerrilla movement. He states that Monje himself actually intercepted well-trained Communist militants who were on their way to join the guerrillas and prevented them from leaving La Paz. Castro argues that this demonstrates that there are men in the Communist ranks who have both the desire and ability to fight, but that their efforts to do so are "criminally frustrated by incapable leaders, charlatans, and tricksters." He goes on to say that leaders such as Monje have turned revolutionary ideas into a "dogmatic opium" for the masses, and that they have discredited the revolutionary organizations of the people by entering into political deals with both the people's foreign and domestic exploiters. These are extremely serious accusations for one Communist to level at another. Yet it is interesting to note that Castro condemns Monje, the individual, rather than Monje, the loyal representative of Moscow and leader of the pro-Moscow Communists in Bolivia. Cuba's dependence upon Moscow obviously prevented him from openly stating this.

What is the full story behind Castro's accusations? How did Monje betray Che, and why did Monje and the other pro-Moscow Communist leaders sabotage Che's guerrilla movement? The answers to these questions provide a remarkable insight into the nature of the mortal struggle that is taking place between the different leftist factions in Latin America today.

It is perhaps best to begin by enumerating the five ways in which Bolivia's pro-Moscow Communist leaders betrayed Che and his guerrilla operation:

(1) They gave Havana false information about the political situation in Bolivia and about the determination of their party to launch a guerrilla operation there.

(2) They prevented young Bolivian Communists, trained in Cuba, from going to join Che's guerrilla force.

(3) They promised Che support which they never gave him.

(4) They prevented the militants in their party from fighting with Che and his comrades.

(5) They provided the Bolivian authorities and the CIA with important information about Che and his guerrilla force.

Each of these moves was an act of betrayal, and together they assured the defeat of Che's operation.

The first and perhaps the most important act of betrayal committed by the pro-Moscow Communist leaders was the false information they gave Havana about Bolivia's revolutionary potential, for it was this information which was instrumental in bringing Che to Bolivia in the first place. The lies and boasting of the Bolivian delegation at the Tricontinental Conference in January, 1966, misled the Cubans into believing that a guerrilla-led uprising in Bolivia would be able to count upon the support of a very strong and revolutionary Communist Party, and that the political conditions in Bolivia favored a Cuban-type revolution.

Monje and his comrades portrayed Bolivia as an anarchic state characterized by tumult, violence, and widespread discontent. They boasted that their party had control over the workers and the peasantry, who, they said, were ready to rise up in arms against the government. They conveyed a picture of Bolivia which was so favorable for carrying out a guerrilla-led insurrection that Che could not possibly have doubted the success of his mission before he arrived in Bolivia. On the basis of the information provided by the pro-Moscow Communists, he was led to believe that once armed actions were started against the government, the peasantry and workers would leave their jobs and farms to go in search of his guerrilla force (as they did during the Cuban revolution). In reality, of course, Che and Castro were deceived by some of the best "con-artists" in Latin America. Monje and his friends had planned a fraudulent guerrilla operation in order to expand their party treasury at Cuba's expense, and when Castro and Che tried to establish a guerrilla force in Bolivia largely on their own, Monje paid them back by sabotaging their efforts.

Since the failure of the guerrilla movement, the pro-Moscow group has denied that they ever informed Cuba that the conditions in Bolivia were favorable for a guerrilla-led revolution. They have claimed in their party newspaper and elsewhere that in fact they warned Havana on a number of occasions that the situation in Bolivia was not appropriate for an armed struggle such as Che planned. The evidence to the contrary is, of course, irrefutable, but this has not deterred the pro-Moscow leadership from making such claims.

Once Monje and the other pro-Moscow Communist leaders learned that Che was in Bolivia organizing a guerrilla movement, they consulted Moscow and, with Soviet encouragement, immediately went to work sabotaging the movement. One of their first acts of overt sabotage was reported by Che in his diary only three weeks after his New Year's Eve meeting with Monje. Che's entry indicates that Monje spoke to three young Bolivian Communists who had been sent from Cuba to fight with his group, and persuaded them not to join the guerrilla movement. Following this incident, Monje notified Castro that he would not allow any members of his party to join the guerrillas in the southeast.

Sometime later, Coco Peredo was in La Paz for the purpose of taking several recruits to the guerrilla camp in Ñancahuazú. Much to their surprise, Coco and these recruits, who were all members of the youth wing of Monje's party, encountered Monje waiting for them at the bus terminal in La Paz. Monje interposed himself between Coco's group and the door of the bus which they were planning to take to the southeast. He forbade the young Communists with Coco from joining the guerrilla movement and assured them he would give their names to the authorities if they refused to do as he said. Although Coco reacted violently and threatened to kill Monje the next time he returned to La Paz, he realized he had no choice but to return to the guerrilla camp alone. Under no circumstances could he afford to take the risk that Monje might inform on the guerrillas at that point in their preparations. As it was, Coco never returned to La Paz, for the guerrillas were discovered by the military soon thereafter, and Coco was never able to leave the combat zone in the southeast. One can imagine that the news of Coco's death six months later was received with some relief by Monje, who is said to have been very frightened by Coco's threats.

As previously mentioned, the leaders of the pro-Moscow party deceived the rank and file of the Party for several months after the initiation of hostilities, leading them to believe that the Party was giving sufficient support to the guerrillas. By deceiving their own members in this way, they were able to prevent the more militant members of the Party, who sympathized with the guerrillas, from going to the southeast to fight alongside Che. When the more militant members of the Party realized that he needed help badly, they demanded that their leaders allow them to go fight with the guerrillas. However, at this point the Party leaders answered that the guerrilla operation was a hopeless failure, and that they could not jeopardize the Party by allowing the militants to participate in an armed struggle that was certain to fail.

In addition to denying Che valuable manpower, the pro-Moscow leaders also denied the guerrilla movement any political support. Kolle, the number two man in the Party hierarchy, promised Che the party's support on several occasions, but, as indicated above, this support never materialized. If the party leaders had not been intent on sabotaging Che's guerrilla operation, they could have greatly assisted the guerrillas in the urban areas by serving as a source of propaganda and information for them. Che's diary indicates that his lack of contact with the cities was a serious shortcoming after the outbreak of hostilities. Within a month after the hostilities began, Che and his men were totally cut off from the outside. The failure of the pro-Moscow group to give the guerrillas the logistical, organizational, informational, and propaganda support they had promised greatly contributed to their isolation.

However, the pro-Moscow leaders not only abandoned Che and his men to their tragic fate, they also insidiously worked to insure their quick demise. This author learned from reliable sources that a full month and a half before the guerrillas were discovered by the army, several middle-level leaders of the pro-Moscow party attempted to sell the CIA and the Bolivian intelligence service information about Che's presence in Bolivia and his preparation of a guerrilla force in the southeast of the country. Convinced that this was just another attempt to sell false information, a common political pastime in Bolivia, both the CIA and the Bolivian authorities rejected the information as absurd and not worthy of further attention. However, shortly after the initiation of hostilities, when the CIA and the Bolivian authorities realized that they had rejected reliable information about the guerrillas almost two months earlier, they re-established contact with the pro-Moscow Communists. This time, the Communist leaders provided them with valuable information about the guerrilla operation, such as its true size, composition, strategy, and sources of support. In other words, there is evidence that the pro-Moscow leaders engaged in the worst kind of treachery in order to sabotage Che's guerrilla operation.

In fact, Óscar Zamora, the leader of the pro-Peking Communists in Bolivia, suggested to the author, during a long conversation about the guerrilla episode, that Jorge Kolle himself worked with the Barrientos regime and the CIA to help defeat the guerrillas. The character of Bolivian politics being what it is, this is entirely possible. Kolle, whose brother is head of the Bolivian Air Force, has the mysterious ability to travel freely, while other Communist leaders, especially the pro-Peking leaders, remain almost continuously in hiding and can travel only clandestinely. Kolle has even been able to obtain legal permission to travel to the Soviet Union. As Zamora suggests, it may well be that Kolle serves as the connecting link between the Bolivian regime and Washington on the one hand, and the orthodox Communists and Moscow on the other. If this is so, his actions with regard to Che's guerrilla movement take on an even greater significance.

However, leaving aside the question of whether or not Kolle worked with the Barrientos regime and the CIA, let us consider the motives behind Monje's and Kolle's efforts to sabotage Che's guerrilla operation. Why were these two Communist leaders so determined to ensure the quick defeat of Che's force? What were they afraid of?

In the first place, it seems clear that Monje and Kolle were acting in accordance with instructions from Moscow. The moment that Moscow learned that Che was preparing a guerrilla movement in Bolivia and that he planned to extend this movement into the neighboring countries, Moscow instructed the leadership of the pro-Moscow group in Bolivia to do everything necessary to ensure the defeat of the guerrilla operation.

The Russians regarded Che's operation in Bolivia as a serious threat to their Latin American policy. If Che succeeded in turning Bolivia into another Vietnam, or even another Congo, Moscow's relations with the existing regimes in Latin America, as well as with Washington, would be seriously threatened. The Soviet Union's policy of promoting closer relations and establishing economic ties with the present regimes in Latin America would be undermined. Moreover, Moscow was afraid the Red Chinese would be the ones to profit from such a situation. Che's sympathy for the Peking line was well known. Therefore, the Russians, as well as Monje and Kolle, were afraid that Che might seek the support of Bolivia's *Maoistas*, and perhaps even place himself at the service of Peking. Consequently, Moscow instructed Monje and Kolle to refuse Che the cooperation he requested, to prevent him from obtaining recruits, and to inform the Bolivian authorities about the entire operation.

Furthermore, both Moscow and the pro-Moscow leaders in Bolivia saw the situation as an excellent opportunity to demonstrate to the Bolivian people and the rest of Latin America that efforts to liberate the masses through armed struggle are impractical, and that there is no other alternative than that advocated by the pro-Moscow Communists, i.e., to struggle within legal bounds. In other words, they reasoned that if the famous Che Guevara himself failed to liberate the Bolivian people by means of his guerrilla movement, then the people of Latin America would have decisive proof that an armed revolution is not the answer. Evidence that this consideration motivated Monje and Kolle is to be found in some of the articles that appeared in their party newspaper following the announcement of Che's capture and death. In evaluating the death of Che and the defeat of his guerrilla operation, these articles state that even though the party leadership had supported the guerrilla movement, they had regarded it from the beginning as an effort which was dramatically divorced from the reality of prevailing conditions in Bolivia. And one particular article, after elaborating on the idea that Che's undertaking was based on a misconception of existing realities, goes on to say that the party leadership decided at the outset of the guerrilla operation that it would "demonstrate the best way for the Bolivians to follow in order to achieve a revolutionary victory."

In addition to the factors mentioned above, it is important to note that neither Monje nor Kolle was willing to take the personal risks or make the sacrifices that involvement in an armed struggle would have entailed. The leaders of the pro-Moscow Communists throughout Latin America are thoroughly bourgeois. They talk a great deal about misery, hunger, and poverty, but they have never known any of these. The salaries they receive from Moscow allow them to live very comfortably, and they enjoy their bourgeois existence too well to want to give it up for the dangerous life of the revolutionary.

Apart from the pro-Moscow Communists, the other left-wing groups in Bolivia knew little or nothing about Che's guerrilla operation until the news broke at the end of March that the army had discovered a guerrilla force in the southeast of the country. In the months that followed, nearly all these groups expressed their general solidarity with the guerrillas. However, not one of them provided Che with any tangible support.

The pro-Peking Communists did not know anything about the guerrillas until they were discovered by the army. In fact, the principal leaders of the pro-Peking group were in prison at the time, and could not have come to Che's assistance even if they had wanted to do so. Óscar Zamora, the top leader of the *Pekinistas*, had been imprisoned in the "leprosarium" at Puerto Moreno for several months when he learned of the guerrillas and the possibility that their leader might be Che Guevara. Today he admits that if he had not been imprisoned and if Che had contacted him personally to ask for his support, he might have been tempted to support the guerrilla operation. However, as it was, the pro-Peking group remained little more than spectators throughout the entire episode. They, of course, made several pronouncements of moral support for the guerrillas after the fighting began, but they also made it clear that they felt the guerrillas lacked the necessary ideological direction. They even expressed the opinion on several occasions that the guerrillas faced the prospect of being annihilated due to their ideological confusion. One document in particular warned the guerrillas that in a revolution there cannot be any type of opportunism, and that the ideology must command the gun rather than the gun commanding the ideology.

There does appear to have been some belated communication regarding the guerrilla operation between Havana and two of Bolivia's leftist groups: Juan Lechín's Revolutionary Party of the Nationalist Left and Hugo Gonzales' Trotskyite Workers Revolutionary Party. On March 23, 1967, Castro sent Che a message in which he stated that Lechín was in Cuba. Castro indicated that he had informed Lechín about the strategic objectives of the Bolivian guerrilla operation and the fact that Che was personally directing it. According to Castro, Lechín was very enthusiastic about the undertaking and promised to give his support in the form of both men and public declarations. The message said that he would secretly re-enter Bolivia within the next month to meet with Che. However, Lechín never returned to Bolivia. A few months later, he was arrested in Chile while traveling under a false Argentina passport. From the safety of Chilean soil he issued a statement in which he said that the guerrillas were fighting to liberate his country from the foreign yoke imposed on it by the traitorous Barrientos regime.

Lechín's motives and behavior are unclear. Perhaps he intended to use Che's guerrilla operation to his own advantage in a bid to seize power. On the other hand, Antonio Arguedas, the high Bolivian official who sent Che's diary to Castro, has stated that the CIA asked him early in 1967 to provide Lechín (who was wanted by the government at the time) with a passport so that he could travel overseas. Arguedas, who was the Minister of Internal Affairs in the Barrientos government, claims he refused the request since Lechín was an avowed enemy of the regime. But why did the CIA want to help Lechín travel overseas? Could it have been that he was working for them?

The situation is further complicated by the fact that the pro-Moscow Communist leader Jorge Kolle, in an interview with a New York Times correspondent in May, 1967, claimed that the guerrilla force in the southeast of Bolivia was composed of militants from Lechín's party, the Trotskyite Workers' Revolutionary Party, and the pro-Peking group. However, Kolle was most likely lying about the association of these groups with the guerrillas in an effort to bring the wrath of the government down upon them, and thus make life more difficult for his party's major left-wing rivals.

A message from Castro to Che dated July 4, 1967, reveals that one of Castro's agents in La Paz had contacted the section of the Workers' Revolutionary Party led by Hugo Gonzales and learned that this faction of the Trotskyites was predisposed to help the guerrillas. In the same message there is also an indication that certain elements within the National Revolutionary Movement were interested in going to Cuba for guerrilla training. However, in the final analysis, neither of these two groups appears to have participated in the guerrilla operation. They were contacted when it was already too late, and it seems unlikely that their leaders ever had any intention of doing anything more than expressing their moral support for the guerrillas. The leaders of these groups, as well as those of other left-wing groups in Bolivia, hoped that the guerrilla operation would create a situation which would lead to the collapse of the Barrientos regime. Consequently, they expressed support for the guerrilla movement not because they identified with its revolutionary objectives, but because they regarded the guerrilla operation as something which would help promote their own more limited objective of toppling the Barrientos regime.

Che's failure to obtain the positive support of Lechín's followers, Gonzales' Trotskyites, or even the more militant elements within the harassed Nationalist Revolutionary Movement insured the total isolation of his movement. Because he preferred to overlook the fact that he was surrounded on all sides by opportunists, charlatans, and cowards, Che left himself open to betrayal by the pro-Moscow Communists and abandonment by those leftist parties who loudly acclaim their revolutionary ideals but never put them into practice. His single-minded determination and devotion to his ideals made him an easy prey for these left-wing opportunists and impostors.

CHAPTER 13

American Involvement in the Guerrilla Episode

American political and economic involvement in Bolivia is extensive. In fact, the Bolivian economy is largely controlled by American interests. The United States is the largest buyer of Bolivia's tin, the country's economic mainstay. In addition, the main sources of capital investment in Bolivia are American, as are the majority of Bolivia's private mining enterprises and the country's largest oil development scheme. Furthermore, the Bolivian government is dependent upon the financial assistance of the United States government, which annually provides the regime with budgetary support in the form of outright grants and low-interest, long-term loans. This support, plus myriad technical assistance and development programs, makes Bolivia the recipient of one of the largest U.S. aid programs in Latin America.

Since the 1952 revolution, the U.S. government has given Bolivia over four hundred million dollars in aid. The motivation behind this extensive expenditure has been largely political, as evidenced in the following statement from a U.S. Senate report published in 1956: "The Department of State, which constantly appraises political, social, and economic developments, has concluded that the Bolivian government is Marxist rather than Communist and has advocated United States support of this regime on the same premise that it advocated support of the preceding military junta—*to prevent displacement by more radical elements* [author's italics]. As this quote indicates, once the U.S. government determined that the post-revolutionary political leadership in Bolivia was leftist rather than Communist (a distinction which American officials usually find difficult to make), the decision was made to support the Bolivian regime, and in particular the more moderate elements in the ruling National Revolutionary Movement. The primary motive was to stabilize the political situation in Bolivia and prevent any further movement to the left, but almost as important was the desire to protect U.S. economic interests in Bolivia.

The American presence in Bolivia has increased notably in recent years. This is particularly true in the southeast, where over one hundred million dollars have been invested by the U.S. government alone, not to mention the amounts invested by Gulf Oil and other American firms interested in opening up the area. This investment has gone into the construction of the Cochabamba-Santa Cruz highway (the only paved, all-weather road in Bolivia) and the Santa Cruz-Corumba railway (which links Santa Cruz with southern Brazil), as well as into sugar mills, oil wells, agricultural improvement projects, farm credit programs, school construction, etc.

The American presence in Bolivia is also visible in the form of hundreds of American missionaries, Peace Corps volunteers, and civilian advisers of one kind or another. It is interesting in this regard to note that Regis Debray has paid tribute to the importance of this pervasive American presence in the rural areas of Latin America by asserting that it has made the establishment of guerrilla movements in these areas more difficult. For example, in his book *Revolution in the Revolution?* Debray states:

As for American imperialism, it has increased its forces in the field, and is making every effort to present itself, not in repressive guise, but in the shape of social and technical assistance. . . . Thousands of Peace Corpsmen have succeeded in integrating themselves in rural areas—some of them by dint of hard work, patience, and at times real sacrifice—where they profit by the lack of political work by left-wing organizations. Even the most remote regions are today teeming with Catholic, Evangelical, Methodist, and Seventh Day Adventist missionaries. In a word, all these close-knit networks of control strengthen the national machinery of domination, and without exaggerating the depth or scope of their penetration, we can say that they have indeed changed the scene. [New York, 1967, p. 53.]

There is little doubt that the American presence in countries such as Bolivia has made life more difficult for revolutionary guerrilla movements. But as important as the extensive American political and economic involvement in these countries is the extent of American military assistance.

Over the last five years, U.S military assistance to Latin America has increased enormously. To date, the United States has spent over *one billion dollars* in equipping and training the armies of thirteen countries in Latin America. One very important by-product of this massive program of military assistance has been the increased influence of the military in Latin American politics. It is no accident, therefore, that over two-thirds of the countries receiving U.S. military aid now have military or military-backed regimes.

In recent years, the main emphasis of American military aid has been placed on increasing the "internal security" capability of the Latin American countries. The U.S. government now recognizes that Latin America is not threatened by overt external aggression. American military assistance, therefore, is no longer directed at promoting hemispheric defense against foreign aggression, but rather toward the suppression of subversion and popular insurrections within the Latin American countries. In accordance with this new policy, the police and armed forces of most of the Latin

American countries have been trained and equipped by the United States to handle anything from student riots to large-scale popular revolts. In addition, Latin American army officers and soldiers have been taught the latest counterinsurgency tactics and given instruction in the administration of "civic action" programs designed to improve their public image. In fact, close to twenty thousand Latin American officers and soldiers have received special counterinsurgency training from the U.S. Army at Fort Gulick in the Panama Canal Zone, and many others have been trained by American military advisory teams stationed in their home countries.

In the case of Bolivia, the armed forces, particularly the officer corps, have been greatly influenced by American military assistance and training. In fact, the present military establishment was created by former president Paz Estenssoro with American advice and equipment in order to serve as a counterweight to the miners' and peasants' militias, which destroyed the traditional army in the 1952 revolution. Under American guidance the new Bolivian Army became the first in Latin America to launch a civic action program aimed at building a favorable image for itself among the general population. This program, involving the construction of schools and roads in the rural areas, was undertaken at the suggestion and with the help of the U.S. Military Assistance and Advisory Group (MAAG) in Bolivia. Evidently, the "civic consciousness" resulting from the introduction of such programs partially explains why the new, American-advised army ousted the elected civilian government in 1964 and placed in power the senior officer most closely associated with the American military advisors, General René Barrientos.

Although a number of journalistic accounts have exaggerated the role played by the U.S. government and American personnel in the defeat of Che's guerrilla operation in Bolivia, a dispassionate analysis of the evidence available reveals that direct American involvement in the entire episode was minimal. Far from pushing the panic button when word was first received of the guerrilla operation in the southeast of Bolivia, the Washington policymakers responded to the situation in a very uncharacteristic manner—they played it cool. Perhaps this response was a result of their determination to avoid another Vietnam, and their awareness that Che's strategy hinged upon involving the U.S. directly in the contest. At any rate, early in the game the decision was made to restrict American assistance to logistics, training, and intelligence. Moreover, the U.S. government found it necessary to persuade the military government of Argentine strongman Juan Carlos Onganía that there was no need for Argentina to intervene in the Bolivian guerrilla operation, despite the ineffectiveness of the Bolivian army and the proximity of the guerrilla operation to Argentina's northern border. As a result of American assurances, the Argentine government merely moved some troops to Argentina's frontier with Bolivia and sent a shipment of arms and ammunition to the Bolivian army. Shortly thereafter, the Peruvian and Brazilian governments did essentially the same thing.

President Barrientos' first response to the discovery of the guerrilla operation in his country was to call immediately upon the U.S. government for additional military aid. However, the U.S. ambassador to Bolivia, Douglas Henderson, was more concerned about the possible overreaction of the Barrientos government to the situation than about the guerrilla threat itself. Among other things, he and his advisers were afraid the Bolivians would indiscriminately start bombing the zone of guerrilla operations and thereby alienate the local civilian population. Washington was anxious not to repeat its mistakes in Vietnam by giving napalm and additional aircraft to the Bolivians. On the other hand, something obviously had to be done, for if the Bolivian Army failed to respond effectively to the guerrilla threat, the guerrillas might succeed in winning popular support or the Barrientos regime might be toppled by elements within the military anxious to find a scapegoat for their failures. Consequently, Washington decided that the Bolivian Army should be given only certain kinds of military equipment and special training in counterguerrilla warfare so as to improve its combat effectiveness.

On April 1, 1967, the first installment of American military equipment arrived in Santa Cruz aboard a U.S. Air Force C-130 cargo plane. Subsequent shipments increased the amount of material assistance to well over five million dollars, but this aid was restricted to light arms, ammunition, communications equipment, and helicopters. Meanwhile, the U.S. government persuaded the Bolivians that their most important need was in the area of training. Consequently, by mid-April plans had already been made for the establishment of a special training camp where U.S. advisers would train a new elite counterinsurgency force. By the end of April, this special training camp was opened at the site of a former sugar mill, named La Esperanza, near Santa Cruz. The training staff sent to organize this camp consisted of fifteen American Green Berets under the command of Major "Pappy" Shelton. This group, most of whom had served in Vietnam, were from the Special Forces garrison in the Panama Canal Zone. Their mission was to train in the shortest time possible a new, crack regiment of 640 Bolivian Rangers who would be capable of carrying out an effective antiguerrilla campaign against Che and his small force. The members of this new regiment were specially recruited from the tropical areas of Bolivia in order to obtain individuals whose prior conditioning would allow them to adapt quickly to the climatic and geographic conditions of the southeast. In addition, the Bolivian officers selected to lead this new regiment had been chosen because of their past training in counterinsurgency at Fort Gulick. One of the most capable officers in the Bolivian army, Colonel José Gallardo, was placed in command of the new regiment and the training camp at La Esperanza.

Major Shelton's orders were to mold an effective counterinsurgency unit out of his raw Bolivian recruits in nineteen weeks, and he and his men were to stay clear of the combat zone at all times. They were to have everything they might need in the way of supplies and equipment. The training program which Major Shelton and his team set up for the new Ranger unit was modeled on that of the Green Berets. However, certain special exercises were tailored to the particular needs of their Bolivian trainees. Working on the assumption that the Bolivian army was one of the worst arnies in Latin America, and that this opinion was shared by many Bolivians themselves, Major Shelton and his staff concluded that one of their most important objectives was to develop a high degree of *esprit de corps* and self-confidence among the Bolivian recruits. Thus, in addition to intensive training in the techniques of counterguerrilla warfare, the Bolivian recruits were also exposed to a number of morale-boosting programs. These included periods during which they spent hours shouting "I'm the toughest" and "I'm the best." Although this may seem somewhat ridiculous, it appears to have been necessary in order to overcome the inbred sense of inferiority and lack of confidence suffered by most of Bolivia's Indian population.

The new Ranger regiment, called Manchego No. 2, completed its special training program by mid-September, less than five months after its formation. Evaluating the caliber of the military unit which passed in review before them at the ceremony marking the termination of their training, Major Shelton and his staff could take pride in having worked a true miracle in military training. The troops who passed before them, wearing green berets and marching smartly with their heads high, were far better than any other unit in the Bolivian armed forces. Unlike their less fortunate comrades already in the field, they were both properly trained and equipped to fight under the conditions of guerrilla warfare. Among the speeches at the passing out ceremony for Manchego No. 2, Colonel Gallardo, the regimental commander, thanked the American advisers for their invaluable assistance and credited them with having created "the new personality" possessed by his troops. This, more than anything else, seems to have been the main American contribution to the military defeat suffered by Che's guerrilla force. Following their training at La Esperanza, the Rangers of Manchego No. 2 were sent into the Vallegrande-La Higuera area, where they rapidly proceeded to eliminate the handful of guerrillas left under Che's command.

While Major Shelton and his team were training the Rangers, the CIA made a determined effort to improve the intelligence capabilities of the Bolivian army and civilian intelligence service.

Pressure was placed on the Minister of Interior, Antonio Arguedas, to accept several CIA agents as "advisers" on security and
intelligence matters in his ministry. Additional agents were at-
tached to the military high command, and two special agents,
Eduardo Gonzales and Félix Ramos, were assigned to the southeast to collect first-hand information on the guerrilla operation.
Because Washington was anxious not to have Americans present in the combat zone and because they naively assumed that
agents of Latin American origin would be less conspicuous in Bolivia, all of the operatives assigned to the guerrilla situation were
Cuban exiles. However, their Cuban accents and phony-sounding
names made them as conspicuous as any of the *gringo* advisers in
the Bolivian government.

Eduardo Gonzales, or Doctor Gonzales, appears to have been responsible for interrogating all the prisoners taken in association
with the guerrilla operation. He was the CIA agent who questioned Regis Debray and to whom Debray appears to have given
information about Che and the guerrilla operation. Gonzales also
interrogated the deserters and the guerrillas taken prisoner during
the last months of the guerrilla operation. Moreover, he went to
La Paz to question Loyola Guzmán and the other members of the
guerrilla urban underground who were arrested in September,
1967. Finally, it was he who questioned Che Guevara in La Higuera and who, together with Félix Ramos, supervised the disposal
of his body.

Félix Ramos was assigned to work with the Bolivian troops in
the field. He was responsible for combat intelligence and for collecting as much information as possible on the guerrilla operation.
Ramos visited every skirmish site and campsite of the guerrillas,
questioned peasants and soldiers who had been taken prisoner by
them, and carefully compiled a comprehensive and detailed dossier
on the entire operation. According to those who had occasion to
meet him, he was much more talkative and friendly than Gonzales, who spoke very little and avoided contact with just about everyone.

Sensationalist claims about how "the CIA got Che" have no factual foundation at all. To be sure, the CIA was ever-present during the Bolivian guerrilla episode; they certainly were determined to see that Che was defeated and, if possible, captured. However, they were not responsible for the failure of Che's guerrilla operation nor for his execution. In fact, the CIA appears to have opposed the idea of executing Che. Purely for professional reasons, they wanted to keep him alive. However, their advice was rejected by the Bolivians, who felt they could not afford to allow the famous revolutionary to live. There is still some question as to whether the CIA took Che's body back to the U.S., or whether they merely supervised its disposal in Bolivia. Nevertheless, this is far from suggesting that it was the CIA that was responsible for "getting Che."

Exaggerated claims have also been made with regard to the use of infra-red aerial cameras in the detection and location of the guerrillas. One journalist in particular has asserted that the mud "Dienbienphu ovens" used by the guerrillas made it possible for the U.S. Air Force to pinpoint their location at all times by using new, highly sensitive heat-detecting cameras in an around-the-clock aerial surveillance of the combat zone. However, after leaving their main camp in the Ñancahuazú area, where they did have a Dienbienphu oven, the guerrillas never stayed anywhere long enough to build another one. In fact, they rarely even built fires. Furthermore, the Bolivian authorities knew at least the general location of the guerrillas throughout the entire period from their initial discovery to their elimination, without having to rely upon such sophisticated American gimmickry as heat-sensing infra-red cameras. For one thing, during the first four months, Che's column clashed with the army on a fairly frequent basis, and it was possible to ascertain simply from these encounters the general location of the guerrillas. Moreover, the army constantly received information about them from the local peasantry. In fact, the irony of the situation is that the Bolivian military knew far more about the guerrillas than the latter knew about the army—the exact reverse of the usual situation in guerrilla warfare.

In sum, the American involvement in Bolivian affairs is extensive, but the American contribution to the military defeat of Che's guerrilla operation was minimal. To be sure, the American-trained Rangers of Manchego No. 2 were responsible for capturing Che and almost completely eliminating his small force in October, 1967. However, Che's guerrilla operation was already defeated prior to the arrival on the scene of the American-trained Rangers. His force had lost over half of its original members and had failed to win any popular support. Moreover, the hostility of the pro-Moscow Communists and the indifference of the other leftist groups in Bolivia, together with the capture of the guerrillas' urban contacts in La Paz, had left Che and the tattered remnants of his original force completely and hopelessly isolated by the time the Rangers entered into combat against them.

CHAPTER 14

The Publication of Che's Diary

ЛЛЛЛЛЛЛЛЛЛЛЛЛЛЛЛЛЛЛЛЛЛЛЛЛЛЛЛ

Perhaps the most incredible aspect of the story surrounding Che's guerrilla operation involves the publication of his campaign diary. Following his capture and execution, the Barrientos government decided to sell Che's diary to the publisher willing to pay the highest price. However, while the Bolivians were negotiating the sale of the diary, the Cuban government mysteriously obtained a copy and released it through a series of publishing houses in Latin America, Europe, and the United States. By publishing the diary before the Bolivians could sell it, the Cuban government was able to score a significant propaganda victory and greatly embarrass the Barrientos regime. Moreover, the question of how the Cubans managed to get a copy of the diary gave rise to serious doubts in Bolivia about the integrity of the government and the armed forces. Clearly, someone in either the government or the military had placed a copy of the "top-secret" diary in Cuban hands.

On July 1, 1968, Che's diary was made public in Havana, and

within a few days it was distributed by pro-Cuban publishers in Chile, Mexico, France, Italy, West Germany, and the United States. A few weeks later, on July 19, Antonio Arguedas, minister of internal affairs in the Barrientos government, fled to Chile and was denounced by General Ovando as the traitor who had provided the Cuban government with a photostatic copy of Che's diary. Bolivians were stunned by the news, and most of the population regarded Arguedas' actions as a national disgrace. Since Arguedas had been Barrientos' right-hand man, the whole affair seriously undermined the public's confidence in the Barrientos regime and within twenty-four hours plunged the country into a grave political crisis that broke apart the coalition of parties which had previously supported Barrientos. At the same time, the three main opposition parties (the Socialist Falange, the National Revolutionary Movement, and the Revolutionary Party of the Nationalist Left) issued a manifesto calling upon the Barrientos government to resign. They also called a mass demonstration in the capital on July 20, which resulted in a violent clash with the police and the death of a captain of the Civil Guard. The leaders of the demonstration were arrested, and Barrientos declared a nationwide state of emergency. He also called upon the peasant syndicates in the Cochabamba area to come to his assistance, and some five thousand armed *campesinos* from the Cochabamba Valley were mobilized and moved to the outskirts of the capital. This appears to have been the turning point in the crisis; soon thereafter Barrientos received expressions of public support from the various military garrisons throughout the country, as well as several important political groups. Ironically, the crisis arising from the publication of Che's diary, and particularly Arguedas' part in the whole affair, came close to toppling the Barrientos regime—something which Che's guerrilla operation never was able to do.

But the Arguedas affair did not end there. Much to everyone's surprise, approximately a month after his flight, Antonio Arguedas returned to Bolivia to stand trial for his actions. In Chile, Arguedas had publically declared that he wanted to return to Bolivia to clear his name. However, most Bolivians assumed Arguedas had received a large sum of money from the Cubans in return for Che's diary, so no one took seriously his announced intention to return home. This made it all the more surprising when he did return to Bolivia, following a month-long odyssey which took him to La Paz via London, New York, and Lima.

On August 17, the day of his return to Bolivia, Arguedas was met at the airport outside La Paz by a heavy police guard and a large crowd of Bolivian and international correspondents. When his plane landed, the reporters attempted to move onto the concrete where the plane was due to halt but they were stopped by the police. However, two officials of the American embassy, carrying cameras, were allowed to pass through the police cordon, and this obvious discrimination gave rise to heated protests from the reporters, who were finally allowed to move closer. As the plane came to a halt and the portable stairways were wheeled into position at the forward and rear doors, a rented car, escorted by several police motorcycles and a jeep, pulled up in front of the forward stairway. After the other passengers on the plane had disembarked via the rear door, Arguedas was escorted out of the front door and down the stairs into the waiting car by two police officials. He was followed by a large number of foreign correspondents who had flown with him from Lima. Arguedas was taken to the Bolivian national airline building, where he was allowed to meet with his wife and one of his sons and then to talk with the waiting crowd of reporters.

The press conference at the airport lasted exactly seventeen minutes before it was abruptly terminated by the director of the Criminal Investigations Division. Arguedas had just begun to reveal some of the activities of the CIA in Bolivia and his former ties with this American spy organization, when the director suspended the conference on the grounds that there were public disturbances in the city and that it was therefore necessary to transport the prisoner to safety immediately. Then, amid protests from both the reporters and Arguedas, the latter was forcibly removed to another room in the building. About five minutes later, a security agent wearing Arguedas' clothing was hurriedly rushed into a car and driven away in the wake of a motorcycle escort. However, the deception failed, and the reporters waited outside the building for Arguedas to reappear. Approximately a half hour later, the director of information of the presidency appeared and admitted to the press that Arguedas was still in the building but that he was prohibited for the time being from making any public declarations. Shortly thereafter, a police jeep arrived, and Arguedas was taken to it under heavy guard. As he reached the jeep, he shouted at the reporters: "I demand that the press conference be continued in order to expose the CIA." He was cut short by a violent effort on the part of his guards to push him into the jeep. They succeeded in forcing him into it and, together with another police vehicle, it immediately sped away in the direction of the city.

Later in the day, Arguedas was taken to the Ministry of Internal Affairs, and upon instructions from the president, he was permitted to meet with the press a second time. This time he was allowed to answer approximately thirty questions during the course of an hour and a half. Afterwards he was returned to his cell in the Criminal Investigations Division and not allowed to meet with the press again.

Arguedas revealed to the press that his association with the CIA had begun in 1964, shortly after the MNR government of Paz Estenssoro was overthrown by the military. At that time, Arguedas was appointed to the high-level administrative post of sub-secretary in the Ministry of Internal Affairs. But two months after his appointment, Colonel Edward Fox, the air attache in the U.S. Embassy, informed Arguedas that if he continued in office, the United States government would suspend all economic assistance to Bolivia and take drastic measures against its government. The reason given was Arguedas' past membership in the Bolivian Communist Party. In order to avoid any trouble, Arguedas resigned. However, several weeks later, he was again contacted by Colonel Fox, who told him the U.S. government might reconsider their opposition to him if he would meet with an American diplomat in Bolivia. Arguedas agreed, and Colonal Fox introduced him to Larry Sterfield, then the head of the CIA in Bolivia. Sterfield suggested to Arguedas that he voluntarily undergo interrogation outside of Bolivia so that it could be determined whether or not he had been a militant member of the Communist Party and whether or not the Party had instructed him to infiltrate the new military regime.

In order to clear himself with the Americans, Arguedas agreed to go to Lima for several days of intensive interrogation by the CIA. In Lima, he was exposed to three days of interviews and interrogation with the use of a lie detector. On the fourth day, he was interrogated while under the influence of drugs. When he recovered, the CIA told him they were convinced he had not been a militant member of the Communist Party, nor had he been instructed by the Party to infiltrate the new government in Bolivia. As far as they were concerned, he was free to resume his duties in the Ministry of Internal Affairs.

Arguedas returned to La Paz and was reappointed to his post in the ministry. However, as time went by, the CIA asked him to provide them with various kinds of information to which he had access in his position. Later on, they told him that they would see that he became the next minister of internal affairs. They promised to praise him in all the right circles and to present him as the ideal person for this important post. Soon articles began appearing in the newspapers concerning the marvelous job Arguedas was doing. In addition, the Americans around President Barrientos began praising Arguedas. The president assumed that Arguedas had become friends with the Americans through his work in the Ministry, and largely because the Americans thought so highly of Arguedas, Barrientos appointed him minister of internal affairs. At that time, the CIA invited Arguedas to visit Washington and gave him sixty-five hundred dollars for traveling expenses. In Washington, they briefed him on the politics of the various Latin American countries and about the revolutionary activities and shortcomings of Fidel Castro's regime in Cuba. Evidently, they wanted to ensure that his outlook on Latin American affairs conformed with theirs.

After he became minister of internal affairs, Arguedas' relations with the CIA assumed a totally different character. According to Arguedas, under the threat of blackmail they forced him to carry out a variety of activities which served their interests. Through him, he claimed, they took control of the most important operations in his ministry, in particular the state intelligence service. This in turn allowed them to infiltrate agents into many of Bolivia's political parties and to control the information presented to the president and the cabinet on matters of internal security. Naturally, this arrangement also gave the CIA access to all of Bolivia's state secrets.

Arguedas also revealed that the CIA gave him money to corrupt various Bolivian leaders. He told the press of an instance in which the CIA gave him twenty-five hundred dollars to obtain information from an important union leader about the contacts he had made on a recent trip to China and various other socialist countries. On this particular occasion, the individual concerned refused to be bought. However, Arguedas made it clear that a good many other individuals were compromised in this manner. Arguedas also claimed that the CIA had charged him with the task of destroying the reputation of the co-director of Bolivia's best newspaper, *Presencia*. It seems that the newspaperman in question had organized a civic group to carry out a campaign of community development in the rural areas. For some reason this greatly alarmed the head of the CIA in Bolivia, and he gave Arguedas money to employ people to paint on the walls around La Paz signs which gave the impression that the newspaperman was organizing his own political party instead of a civic group. The CIA also gave Arguedas money to further discredit the newspaperman by involving him in *un escándalo de faldas* ("a scandal of skirts").

According to Arguedas, during the time he was in office the CIA intervened extensively in Bolivian affairs. They spread information which undermined the government's attempts to negotiate credit in France. They recruited agents from, and infiltrated, nearly all of the major political parties and government agencies in the country. They also gave assistance to the military or political careers of those persons whom they were interested in advancing.

Moreover, it is extremely interesting to note that the head of the CIA mission in Bolivia asked Arguedas to give Juan Lechín (the outlawed popular leader of the Revolutionary Party of the Nationalist Left) a passport under a false name so that he could leave the country and travel abroad. Although Arguedas did not say why the CIA wanted to help Lechín leave the country, it seems clear that Lechín had made some kind of deal with the CIA.

Because Lechín was an enemy of the Barrientos regime and a wanted man, Arguedas refused to give the CIA the passport. His obstinacy created friction between him and the CIA chief, which increased as time went by. Apparently, his relations with the CIA were further estranged when, under his orders, the Bolivian police broke up an underground spy network which they thought was being run by the pro-Peking Communists. Following the announcement by Arguedas that the government had uncovered a pro-Peking spy network, he was angrily informed by Hugo Murray, the CIA agent who worked most closely with him, that the network belonged to the CIA. The CIA, not content with controlling the Bolivian intelligence apparatus, had organized their own intelligence network under the camouflage of a pro-Peking operation.

When Che's guerrillas were discovered in the southeast, the head of the CIA mission in Bolivia called Arguedas and informed him that he was sending him some "advisers." According to Arguedas, the CIA chief told him that their presence was required because of the ineffectiveness of Bolivia's security agents. A few days later, four Cuban exiles arrived and assumed "advisory" positions in Arguedas' ministry. Within a short time, the Bolivian officials in the ministry began to refer to these Cubans as *gusanos* (worms), the name commonly used by pro-Castro Cubans to refer to opponents of the regime. One of these *gusanos*, who went by the name of Gabriel García García, proceeded to operate completely on his own. Without consulting Arguedas, he set up two houses of interrogation where Bolivians suspected of working with the guerrillas were brought for questioning. Arguedas did not find out about this until he received reports that Bolivian citizens were being interrogated and in some cases tortured by foreign agents at both places. He became furious and notified the CIA that he would not permit this sort of thing to continue.

According to Arguedas, the situation grew worse a few months later, when the CIA asked him to influence the outcome of a lawsuit brought against an American mining company by the state-owned Bolivian Mining Corporation. Arguedas claims the CIA told him it was necessary, in order to guarantee private initiative in Bolivia, that the Court decide in favor of the American mining firm. However, it seems that Arguedas had received specific instructions from the president to ensure that the Court's decision was correct. As a result, Arguedas informed the public prosecutor that if any irregularities occurred in the suit against the American firm, he would bring the prosecutor before the Supreme Court. In the end, the decision, reached in accordance with the law, went against the American company. This indicated to the CIA that Arguedas was escaping from their control.

On June 13, 1968, Arguedas was celebrating his birthday, when he received a call from the head of the CIA mission in Bolivia, who told Arguedas to come to his house so that he could congratulate him. This offended Arguedas; he considered the call an affront and did not go to the house of the CIA chief. However, the next day, one of the CIA agents came to Arguedas and told him that his chief was upset over the fact that Arguedas had failed to visit him. He said that his superior had a present for Arguedas which had been sent from the United States and that he should go to receive it. Reluctantly, Arguedas decided to go, in order to avoid any more friction with the Americans.

Arguedas received the present, chatted for a while with his host, and then returned to the ministry, where he opened the package. It contained a pistol, a belt and holster, and three photographs. One of the photographs was of Fidel Castro, the second was of Che Guevara, and the third was a photograph of Raul Castro receiving ammunition from a Cuban guerrilla. Arguedas interpreted these items as a blackmail threat. He believed this was the CIA's way of telling him that if he did not do exactly as they ordered him to do in the future, they would have him denounced as a Castroite. This infuriated Arguedas, and in the heat of the moment he resolved to take vengeance against the CIA. Under the glass top on his desk was a European address which had been found on one of the guerrillas killed in La Higuera. This address had been used by them as a terminal from which communications could be sent to Cuba. Arguedas wrote this address on a large manila envelope and placed inside a set of photographic negatives of Che's diary which he had had made some time earlier when the CIA gave him Che's diary. Inside the envelope he inserted a brief note to Fidel Castro in which he said that he was a friend of the Cuban Revolution and that he was sending him a set of photographic negatives of Che Guevara's diary as a present. He said that Fidel could publish it whenever he pleased and that he did not want any financial compensation.

After he had mailed the diary, Arguedas informed President Barrientos of the disturbing present he had received from the CIA chief. He asked Barrientos to relieve him of his duties in order to avoid any further difficulties with the Americans. However, Barrientos refused to accept Arguedas' resignation and promised to look into the matter personally. The following day, Arguedas called the head of the CIA mission and demanded an explanation. On the phone, the CIA chief told him that it was all a "joke." The pistol was intended as a present, and the photographs were meant to be used as targets.

A little over two weeks after Arguedas had mailed his copy of Che's diary to Castro, the photographer who had been employed by Arguedas many months earlier to make a photographic copy of the diary came to him and said that he knew Arguedas was the one who had given Castro Che's diary. The photographer had just seen the Cuban edition of Che's diary, which contained photographs of several pages of the real diary, and he had recognized these illustrations as having been made from the negatives he had given Arguedas. Later the same day, Arguedas received an urgent telephone call from the CIA agent named García García, who said that he had some very important information to give Arguedas and told him to meet him immediately at a certain bridge in La

Paz. However, Arguedas was suspicious. He concluded that the CIA had discovered he had given Castro his copy of Che's diary, and that they were now intent upon having him gunned down in the streets and placing the blame on leftist terrorists or one of the opposition parties. Since he had no intention of dying this way, he did the only thing left for him to do—he fled the country.

Arguedas, accompanied by his brother, escaped to Chile by driving a jeep overland across the *altiplano* to the Chilean border. There he asked the Chilean authorities for political asylum (Chile and Bolivia do not have diplomatic relations) and informed them that the CIA was intent upon eliminating him. The Chilean police immediately placed Arguedas under guard and took him to Santiago. However, much to Arguedas' surprise, he discovered that the Chilean police and the CIA were working hand in hand. In Santiago, he was questioned by a Chilean police official named Señor Zuñiga and a CIA agent named Nicolas Leondiris (one of the agents who had interrogated Arguedas in Lima four years earlier). According to Arguedas, Zuñiga told him that no one would believe his story about the CIA and that he could make a sizable fortune if he publicly accused General Ovando of having sold Che's diary to Cuba. Zuñiga also told Arguedas that there had been a coup d'état in Bolivia and that the new president was General Marcos Vásquez. (It is interesting that about a month later General Vásquez did make an unsuccessful attempt to seize power from Barrientos.) Unless Arguedas denounced Ovando, Zuñiga assured him that they would turn him over to General Vásquez, who would surely have him shot. However, Arguedas refused to believe that a coup d'état had taken place in Bolivia, and he refused to denounce anyone. He told Zuñiga and Leondiris that he was determined to follow Che Guevara's example and live by the truth.

Leondiris then told Arguedas that if he went ahead with his plans to expose the CIA's activities in Bolivia, the CIA would in fact engineer a coup d'état in Bolivia and see that his house and family were attacked. These threats frightened Arguedas, but he still refused to slander any of the Bolivian leaders. Instead, he made a deal with the CIA. In return for not exposing the CIA's activities in Bolivia, Arguedas exacted a guarantee from Leondiris that the CIA would take no action against his family or the Bolivian government. Moreover, Arguedas also demanded that the CIA withdraw from Bolivia all of their agents, as well as the AID advisory personnel in the various ministries of the Bolivian government.

According to Arguedas, the CIA agents never had any intention of carrying out their end of the bargain, and he knew it. They were merely playing along with him until they could either buy him off, discredit him, or eliminate him. He, on the other hand, was playing for time and the opportunity to return to Bolivia. As for the Chileans, they wanted Arguedas to leave Chile as soon as possible. Zuñiga told Arguedas that Chile needed American aid and that they were afraid to permit him to stay in Chile because he might explode at any moment and publicly accuse the Americans of all kinds of barbarities, thereby placing Chile in an embarrassing position vis-á-vis the U. S. Government. As a result, both Zuñiga and Leondiris suggested to Arguedas that he go to either Cuba or France. Arguedas, however, knew that if he went to either of these countries, whatever he might later say about the CIA could easily be dismissed as anti-American propaganda. Therefore, he insisted on going to New York and finally got Leondiris to obtain a visa for him. Arguedas assumed that New York would be the safest place for him to go since the CIA would not dare assassinate him in the United States. Leondiris, on the other hand, made arrangements for himself and Arguedas to fly to New York via London, probably with the hope of persuading Arguedas to go from London to either France or Cuba.

Arguedas reached London escorted by Leondiris and a Chilean police agent named Óscar Pizarro. At London airport, they were isolated from the waiting reporters and television cameras and kept incommunicado for several hours by the British immigration authorities. According to Arguedas, he asked Leondiris why they were being detained and why, if their agreement was to go to New York, they could not simply take the next flight to New York. At this point, Arguedas claims Leondiris told him that even the CIA

had its problems. A short time later, a British official handed Arguedas a note in Spanish which stated that he had entered the country illegally and could stay for only three days. Then his passport
was stamped and he and his two escorts were led to a taxi waiting
outside. The taxi took the three of them to the Apollo Hotel,
where they registered under their middle names rather than their
surnames. Arguedas could not speak English and was completely
disoriented. He knew something was up and decided to play the
situation by ear. It was not long before Leondiris again approached
him about going to France. He refused, fearing that he would
have difficulty returning to Bolivia once he was in France and insisted that they take him to New York as originally planned. Meanwhile, there was increasing pressure from the House of Commons
for Arguedas to be brought out of hiding and allowed to speak.

Leondiris was afraid Arguedas might tell the British public
about the CIA's activities in Bolivia, in spite of the threats he had
made earlier to keep Arguedas from talking in Chile. With both
the British Foreign Office and the Cuban Embassy demanding to
speak with Arguedas, Leondiris insisted that Arguedas give him
proof that he could be trusted not to break their earlier agreement.
Because Arguedas wanted to return to Bolivia, he assured Leondiris that he would carry out his end of the bargain. As proof of his
good intentions, he told Leondiris where he had hidden a complete account of Che's death given to him by Sergeant Jaime
Terán, the soldier chosen to kill Che. Once this was verified, Leondiris allowed Arguedas to speak by phone with the British Foreign
Office and the Cuban and Bolivian embassies. To all three, Arguedas made it clear that he was irrevocably determined to return to
Bolivia immediately in order to stand trial for his actions.

Although Arguedas wanted to return to Bolivia directly from
London, he claims the CIA prevailed upon him to go to New
York first. Apparently, the CIA still believed they could persuade
Arguedas to give up his plan to return to Bolivia. Arguedas encouraged them in this hope in order to keep them from taking drastic
action against him. It is not clear what took place once Arguedas
reached New York. He spent several days there and then managed

to board a flight to Lima, Peru. Evidently, he must have deceived the CIA into believing he was going to stay in Lima or they would never have allowed him to go there. On the other hand, perhaps by this time the CIA was no longer terribly worried about what he might say. They had by this time withdrawn their advisers from the Bolivian Ministrỹ of Internal Affairs and replaced all the CIA personnel in Bolivia known to Arguedas. Moreover, they had successfully planted a considerable amount of information in the Latin American press which depicted Arguedas as either a traitor or a madman. Thus, they probably assumed that anything Arguedas might say about the CIA's activities in Bolivia would be rejected by the general public as the lies of a disreputable politician. At any rate, Arguedas managed to reach Lima, and much to everyone's surprise he proceeded with his announced intention to return to Bolivia.

When Arguedas reached Lima, he says that he discovered for the first time what the CIA had been doing to blacken his image since his departure from Bolivia a month earlier. He found that the Latin American press was presenting him as an incoherent, half-crazy politician who had received a large sum of money from the Cuban govenment for Che's diary. Arguedas also learned from reading some Bolivian newspapers that the CIA had not fulfilled its part of the agreement. That is, he discovered that there had not been any withdrawal of the American advisory personnel in the various ministries of the Bolivian government. At this point, Arguedas apparently called a CIA contact in Lima and informed him that because the CIA had not fulfilled its agreement with him he therefore felt free to publicly expose its activities in his country. He then informed the Bolivian embassy and the press that he was returning to La Paz within the next few days. From this point on, Arguedas was under constant guard by the Peruvian police and was followed everywhere he went by a growing throng of reporters.

Shortly before his departure from Lima, Arguedas held a press conference in which he denied having received any compensation for giving Che's diary to the Cubans. He also denounced the CIA.

He said that he had kept quiet until this point because he had made an agreement with the CIA in which they were to leave his country in return for his silence. He said that he had also demanded that all the American advisory personnel in Bolivia be withdrawn, and that in the future if the Americans wanted to aid the Bolivian government they should do so on a government-to-government basis. Since the CIA had failed to comply with these conditions, Arguedas told the reporters that he was determined to return to Bolivia and tell the truth about the CIA's involvement in Bolivian affairs.

When he arrived in Bolivia, Arguedas further elaborated on his reason for returning home. He claimed that he had returned in order to clear his conscience and face the consequences of his past actions. His exact words were: "I am not looking for publicity. I only want to tell the truth about everything that occurred in my career as sub-secretary and minister of government, and alert not only the present government of Bolivia, but all the governments of Latin America, as to how North American imperialism undermines their intelligence services in order to introduce errors, to distort, to present a completely different picture of reality, to obstruct their economic relations with other states, and finally to keep them under its control." He said he had returned in order to regain his personal dignity by telling the truth at the moment when it was most appropriate to do so. In this regard, he reminded the reporters of the fact that he had been the favorite of both the Americans and the most reactionary elements in the country prior to his sending Che's diary to Castro, and that he had given up a promising political career because of his disgust over the way in which American political and economic interests had undermined Bolivia's national sovereignty.

At the press conference following his return to Bolivia, Arguedas refuted the suggestion that he had give a copy of Che's diary to Castro because he was a Castroite. He denied being either a Castroite or a Communist and stated that he was a nationalist first and a Marxist second. With regard to the accusation that he had received a large sum of money for the diary, Arguedas angrily retorted that this was another one of the CIA's insidious attempts to discredit him by slander. He argued that if it had been money he was after, it would have been unnecessary for him to sell Che's diary to the Cubans. Arguedas pointed out that as minister of internal affairs he could have made a fortune in bribes from the Americans if he had wanted to do so. He said he had documents hidden outside the country which, among other things, proved that an American engineering firm (which he named) had offered him a bribe of one and a half million dollars to see that they were awarded a government contract for the construction of two new highways. In other words, he argued that he had rejected bribes of much greater amounts than the five hundred thousand dollars it was rumored he had received from the Cubans.

When asked whether he was not afraid that the CIA would have him assassinated, Arguedas answered that if the CIA wanted to send some "patriot" to shoot him in his cell, they were welcome to do it. However, he said that he expected them to continue their efforts to discredit him, and that there was nothing that could be done to stop the machinery they had set in motion to do this. In support of this assertion, he recounted how he had planted an article for the CIA in the Bolivian press which falsely reported that Tania had been a Soviet spy operating under orders to sabotage Che's guerrilla operation. He predicted that articles slandering him would continue to appear in the Latin American press. Nevertheless, he said that he was content with having told the truth even if no one believed him.

Arguedas expressed the opinion that among nearly all the political groups in Bolivia there was a growing awareness of the insidious role being played by the United States in the political and economic life of the country. Moreover, he said that the disgrace of Bolivia's dependence upon the United States was contributing to increasing anti-American feeling and that the moment would come when the national conscience would no longer tolerate American interference in Bolivia's internal affairs. In fact, he predicted that Latin America would turn into another Vietnam if American imperialism continued to manipulate the governments, officials, and institutions of the Latin American countries in accordance with its own selfish interests.

Several times during his discussions with the press, Arguedas expressed his faith in the young leaders of Bolivia's small Christian Democratic Party, whom he characterized as the hope of the country. He exhorted all Bolivians to listen to these young leaders and to unite behind them in defending Bolivia's national dignity and sovereignty. However, he made it quite clear that he was opposed to a forcible overthrow of the current regime. He said that coups lend themselves to CIA manipulation, and that the group which sucessfully brings off a coup usually ends up being more dependent upon the CIA than its predecessor. For this reason, he said that the only alternative was a general election administered by an impartial and autonomous commission composed of honest and respected civic leaders. But even this, according to Arguedas, was no guarantee against CIA interference. He said the CIA had manipulated many elections in Latin America and that several CIA agents had even bragged to him about the CIA's influence over the national elections in the U.S. itself.

The Arguedas affair is one consequence of Che's guerrilla operation which Che himself never could have foreseen. Arguedas' actions shook the Barrientos regime more than did Che's guerrilla activities, which strengthened Bolivia's national unity. By calling into question the integrity of the government and the armed forces, Arguedas' actions weakened Bolivia's national unity and the public's confidence in the existing political system. Moreover, Arguedas' return to Bolivia and his revelations about the nature of the CIA's interference in Bolivian affairs have called into question the role of the United States in that country. In fact, the Arguedas affair should provoke Americans to ask some very serious questions about the nature of their country's involvement in the domestic affairs of the Latin America countries.

The significance of what Arguedas has said about the CIA's involvement in Bolivia and Latin America as a whole must be comprehended in terms of America's professed foreign policy goals of advancing democracy and democratic ideals throughout the world.

If what Arguedas has said is true—and most informed Bolivians believe much if not all of what he has said—then it seems clear that the U.S. is not advancing democracy in Latin America, and that there is sufficient justification for labeling the United States an imperialist power. In fact, it would appear that the United States is helping Latin America's revolutionaries by providing them with a genuine focal point for popular discontent. However, the sordid picture which Arguedas has given of the CIA's Mafia-like intimidation, blackmail, and subversion of supposedly friendly governments is not one the average American will want to believe. To do so would require that he face the fact that his country is not the great and noble force in the world that he imagines it to be.

Following his press conference in the Ministry of Internal Affairs the day of his return to Bolivia, Arguedas was placed in confinement and not allowed to make any further statements to the press. However, within a few months he was released from prison as a result of the Bolivian high court's decision that it did not have the authority to try him. According to the high court, the Bolivian legislature was the only body competent to try a former minister of state for acts of treason committed while in office. Due to the court's decision, Arguedas was released from prison pending action by the legislature. Within a short time after his release, several attempts were made on his life. Twice bombs were thrown at him, and on June 6, 1969, he and a Spanish journalist accompanying him were machinegunned while walking on the street in La Paz. Both Arguedas and the journalist escaped with minor wounds. However, Arguedas was hospitalized for almost a month, and following his release from the hospital, he immediately sought asylum in the Mexican embassy. In a statement which he gave to the press at the time, he explained that his intentions were to leave Bolivia and go to Mexico. He said that he had decided to leave the country because of the increasing political instability in Bolivia following the death of President Barrientos (who had just been killed in the crash of his personal helicopter) and due to the recent attempts upon his life. He gave as an additional reason the failure of the government to take any action whatsoever against the agents of American imperialism at work undermining Bolivia's national sovereignty. The circumstances surrounding Arguedas' flight and return to Bolivia are so bizarre that it would be foolish to try to predict what will happen to him next.

CHAPTER 15

The Cult of Che

ப௱௱௱௱௱௱௱௱௱௱௱௱௱௱௱௱௱௱ா

Today, posters and placards displaying Che's portrait and the slo-
gan "Che lives" appear in student dormitories and at student demonstrations in almost every major city in the world. The Che that
one sees on these posters and placards is a heroic figure, with the
unmistakable beard, beret, and piercing eyes that everyone now as-
sociates with this legendary revolutionary. However, the haunting face that peers out from these mass-produced portraits somehow seems to combine in one human countenance all the races
of mankind. His eyes and moustache appear Asiatic, while the
darkness of his complexion seems Negroid, and the shape of
his nose and cheeks distinctively European. Perhaps this partially
explains why he has become the idol of students and radical intellectuals in every continent, and why, for example, his face is the
only white one to appear on posters alongside those of Muham-
mad Ali and Malcolm X in the black ghettos of the United States.

Since his death, Che has become a popular hero and a symbol
of rebellion on a world-wide scale. In a sense, a cult has developed
around his romantic image. The reasons for this are of considerable importance, for they tell us a great deal about the significance

of the example which Che has given young revolutionaries around the world. It is no accident that young Marxist leaders in Europe such as Rudi Dutschke and Dany "the Red" Cohn-Bendit are admirers of Che. (In fact, Dutschke, the German student leader who was almost killed by a gunman, has even baptized his son "Che.") These young rebels punctuate almost every sentence with Che's famous dictum, "The duty of every revolutionary is to make the revolution." They believe, as did Che, that revolutions are made by people who are willing to act, not by those who are waiting for the appropriate "objective conditions" or for orders from Moscow or Peking. It is interesting in this regard to note that the East European Communist press has referred to these young leftists as "Guevarist-Trotskyite-Maoist hippies." However, such attacks are a matter of little importance to young leftist leaders like Dutschke and Cohn-Bendit, who regard Guevara's activist position as an alternative to the overly dogmatic and bureaucratic party lines of the more orthodox Marxists.

Because of his undaunted and fiercely independent revolutionary idealism, Che has also become the idol of the New Left in the United States and Great Britain, the bulwarks of bourgeois democracy. Students at the London School of Economics and Political Science, one of the most hallowed of Britain's institutions of higher education, greet each other with the salutation "Che"; in the United States, buttons, sweatshirts, and posters with Che's face call forth his memory at anti–Vietnam-war rallies and student demonstrations at universities and colleges from one end of the country to the other.

In Latin America, where Che gave his life fighting for what he believed in, his name has become a battle-cry among leftist students, intellectuals, and workers. His death at the hands of the Bolivian Army made him an instant martyr for all those who are opposed to the oligarchical regimes and glaring social injustices which plague their troubled continent. In spite of the present popularized image of Che, many Latin Americans remember and admire him for his uncompromising intellectual conviction, his sensitivity to the plight of Latin America's exploited masses, and his heroic commitment to his ideals. In their estimation, he truly belongs to them, and deserves to be elevated to the status of Simón Bolívar, José de San Martín, and Emiliano Zapata. Although they have little in common, prominent Latin American figures such as former Argentine dictator Juan Perón and liberal Brazilian archbishop Helder Cámara have praised Che highly, the latter warning that the armed struggle Che advocated is the only alternative unless the present Latin American governments enact long-overdue basic social reforms.

In Cuba, Che has been elevated to the highest position in Cuba's pantheon of revolutionary heroes. Less than a week after Castro acknowledged that Che had indeed been killed by the Bolivians, hundreds of thousands of Cubans silently filled Havana's Plaza de la Revolución to listen tearfully to Fidel as he told dozens of anecdotes about Che and praised Che's intellectual and military virtues. Backed by a huge portrait of Che and flanked by Cuban flags, the Cuban leader gave notice of the importance the Cuban regime planned to give to Che's revolutionary example. Near the end of his tribute to his fallen comrade, Fidel said:

> If we ask ourselves how we want our revolutionary fighters, our militants, and our men to be, then we must answer without any hesitation: They should be like Che! If we ask ourselves how we want the men of future generations to be, we must say: They should be like Che! If we ask how we desire to educate our children, we should say without hesitation: We want our children to be educated in the spirit of Che! If we want a model of man that does not belong to this age but the future, from the heart I say that this model, without a spot on his conduct, or his attitudes, or his actions, is El Che! And when one talks of proletarian internationalism and looks for an example, that example, above all others, is the example of Che!

Today, the Cuban regime is in fact educating the young generation in the spirit of Che. His picture is in every Cuban school, and Cuba's schoolchildren learn by heart quotations from his writings and his letters. For example, tens of thousands of young Cubans now memorize this paragraph from Che's farewell letter to his children: "Grow up as good revolutionaries. Study hard so that you will have command of the techniques that permit the domination of nature. Remember that the revolution is what is most important and that each one of us, alone, is worth nothing. Above all, always remain capable of feeling deeply whatever injustice is commited against anyone in any part of the world. This is the finest quality of a revolutionary." For a regime that wishes to instill a revolutionary tradition in its young, no better example could be chosen. Thus, the words of Che Guevara are on the lips of tens of thousands of young Cubans, and Che is put before them as the model of "the twenty-first-century man."

However, the Cuban leaders are disturbed by the fact that Che has become a "pop hero" in the United States and Western Europe. The commercialization of his image through the marketing of shirts, handkerchiefs, and towels imprinted with his picture, and the distortion of his revolutionary example by American and European movie producers, has greatly alarmed them. As a pop hero, Che is depicted as either a romantic adventurer or a modern-day leftist Robin Hood. This is not the heroic revolutionary figure that the Cubans want put forward as the model of the twenty-first-century man. To them, the romantic adventurer image is just as denigrating as the image of Che held by his avowed enemies, who regard him as either a fanatical anarchist or a Communist renegade.

In one way or another, it seems clear that Che has become a popular hero on a world-wide scale. The phenomenon of hero worship and the process by which individuals become heroes has always been something of a mystery. In all times and places there appears to be a need for heroes. However, in revolutionary times such as these, this need seems greatest. Men everywhere see the societies around them undergoing revolutionary change. Most are frightened of the future which these changes will bring, while others look to the uncertain future with hope. Both need the assurance that man can control his fate and shape the future according to his desires. They sometimes find this assurance in the words and deeds of an exceptional man, whose courage and individual efforts to shape the future according to his ideals, even if seemingly unsuccessful, give them inspiration. Perhaps this is why Che has become a hero for the youth in our times.

Che was a man who had the courage to act in accordance with his ideals. He had the conviction to give his life fighting for a world which he believed he could help bring into being. It is little wonder that he is admired and even worshipped for this. As a Latin American priest said shortly after Che's death: "To pass one's life in the jungle, ill-clothed and starving, with a price of $5,000 on his head, confronting the military power of imperialism, and on top of that, sick with asthma, exposing himself to death by suffocation if the bullets did not cut him down first, a man, who could have lived regally, with money, amusements, friends, women, and vices in any of the great cities of sin; this is heroism, true heroism, no matter how confused or wrong his ideas might have been. Not to recognize this is not only reactionary, but stupid." As this priest pointed out so well, Che's exceptional devotion to the realization of his ideals was truly heroic, and it would be foolish not to recognize this. It follows that those who recognize the heroism in his character and actions cannot help admiring Che, regardless of whether or not they agree with his particular brand of revolutionary idealism. Che was and is a hero to all who admire and are inspired by sincere idealism and exceptional human courage.

CHAPTER 16

Did Che Fail?

⎍⎍⎍⎍⎍⎍⎍⎍⎍⎍⎍⎍⎍⎍⎍⎍⎍⎍⎍⎍⎍⎍⎍⎍⎍⎍⎍⎍⎍⎍

There are those on both sides of the political spectrum who argue that the failure of Che's guerrilla operation in Bolivia clearly indicates that all efforts to carry out a successful armed revolution in Latin America are futile. They claim that Che's failure in Bolivia disproves his theory of revolutionary guerrilla warfare and that his death marks the beginning of the end for all revolutionary movements in Latin America. However, there are those who take just the opposite position. They say that Che may have failed in the short run but that in the long run his cause will succeed. For them, Che's defeat in Bolivia was merely the loss of one battle in a much larger war against the forces of American imperialism and the indigenous ruling oligarchies. They argue that other young revolutionaries, inspired by Che's sacrifice, will now carry on the cause for which he gave his life. Thus, the question is, did Che fail?

If we focus for a moment on the less problematic ramifications of Che's death in Bolivia, we can perhaps acquire a better perspective on the problem. For example, one thing is certain: Che's operation in Bolivia has exposed to full view the true nature of the orthodox Communists in Latin America and the profound differences between them and the pro-Cuban revolutionaries. It is clear that for both the pro-Moscow and pro-Peking Communists the party organization has become an end in itself. It is also clear that the fragmentation of the left in Latin America and the sectarian in-fighting between the various leftist groups, is probably the major obstacle to revolution. Moreover, the duplicity and treachery practiced by the pro-Moscow Communists, who would rather collaborate with the existing oligarchies than assist leftist revolutionaries, is now widely recognized, thanks to the publication of Che's Bolivian diary.

The publication of Che's diary, along with the prologue written by Fidel Castro, unmasked the pro-Moscow Communist leaders in Bolivia. In fact, the rank and file of Bolivia's pro-Moscow party, once they had learned of Mario Monje's betrayal of Che's guerrilla operation, demanded and obtained his resignation. In addition, Óscar Zamora, the leader of the pro-Peking group in Bolivia, publicly condemned the pro-Moscow Communists in an open letter published in both of Bolivia's leading newspapers. The letter said in part: "The publication of Che's campaign diary confirms once again and definitively what our party has sustained all along, accusing, as it does, the 'creole revisionists,' led by Mario Monje and Jorge Kolle, as the direct authors of the most repugnant betrayal in the history of our country's social struggle." Throughout Latin America, the publication of Che's diary has led to the open condemnation of the pro-Moscow Communists by more militant leftists. Thus, the Bolivian episode has focused attention on the counterrevolutionary position taken by all those who adhere to the Moscow line. In view of this fact, it is hard to imagine any revolutionary group ever again trusting the pro-Moscow Communists.

As a result of Che's death and the publication of his diary, it is now clear that any group determined to bring about an armed revolution in Latin America must consider the orthodox Communists to be as great a threat as the repressive forces of the ruling political elites. The pro-Moscow Communists have chosen to make bedfellows of the national bourgeoisie, and in their desire to enjoy the benefits of "peaceful coexistence" they have become as interested in preventing revolutionary insurrections as their bourgeois allies. What effect this will have upon the fortunes of the pro-Moscow parties in Latin America is difficult to determine at this point. However, one thing is sure: the pro-Moscow Communists can be counted out as a revolutionary force in Latin American politics.

Regis Debray appears to have given us the best basis for determining the long-run significance of both Che's death and the defeat of his guerrilla operation in Bolivia. In *Revolution in the Revolution?* he wrote that "for a revolutionary, failure is a springboard" and "as a source of theory it is richer than victory [since] it accumulates experience and knowledge." What Debray says appears to be true in the case of Che's guerrilla operation in Bolivia. But, ironically, the lessons to be learned from the defeat of Che's operation in Bolivia tend to refute Debray's *foco* theory of revolutionary warfare. This is not to say that armed insurrection is impossible in Latin America, but rather that it cannot be successful if it is conceived in the manner Che and Debray have advocated.

Isolated guerrilla *focos* without a mass base of support, no matter how determined and well trained the guerrillas may be, cannot defeat the repressive regimes in Latin America today. This is not what happened in Cuba, and it will not happen in any of the Latin America countries. Castro's guerrilla movement would not have succeeded without the organized support of militant groups in the cities, universities, towns, and sugar plantations. The failure of Che's guerrilla operation in Bolivia clearly reveals that without political support in the urban areas and a broad base of mass support among the peasantry, a guerrilla movement can expect only defeat. The defeat of Che's guerrilla operation, and the faulty foundation of Debray's theorizing, stem from what might be called a kind of military reductionism. This reduces popular revolution merely to a special form of guerrilla warfare and emphasizes the military aspects of the armed struggle against oligarchical rule to the virtual exclusion of the political dimension, when in fact the latter is the more important of the two.

The defeat of Che's guerrilla operation in Bolivia does not indicate that an armed revolution is futile in Latin America or that more peaceful measures are more appropriate for bringing about meaningful social and economic reforms. As long as the existing political elites continue to indefinitely postpone badly needed reforms in their societies, the probability of popular insurrection remains high. Moreover, the repressive measures used by most of the ruling elites to obstruct peaceful efforts aimed at bringing about basic reforms dictate the resort to non-peaceful and extra-legal means.

The Alliance for Progress was supposed to provide a peaceful alternative to violent revolution in Latin America by promoting democracy and socio-economic development through the medium of U.S. assistance. However, most informed observers today generally agree that the Alliance has failed miserably in these respects. Apart from beefing up Latin America's military forces, most of the money that the U.S. has pumped into Latin America over the last five years has been used to refinance the previous debts of the Latin American governments and balance their budgets. Very little of the total amount of U.S. aid has actually gone into reform programs of any sort. Instead American aid has merely served to support the status quo and those who are opposed to major social and economic reforms because these would conflict with their vested interests and privileges.

The failure of Che's guerrilla operation in Bolivia will not deter further efforts to bring about meaningful change through armed struggle. In fact, Che's defeat has helped to clarify for revolutionaries what must be done in order to organize a successful armed insurrection. The basic shortcoming of his operation, as well as that of the various guerrilla movements that have been organized elsewhere in Latin America, was the lack of a mass political organization capable of mobilizing political support for the guerrillas in both the rural and urban areas.

A guerrilla *foco* is not sufficient. The Bolivian situation has shown that unless a guerrilla operation is combined with mass mobilization of the peasantry and political support from organized elements in the urban areas, it will be isolated and wiped out by government troops trained in American counterinsurgency tactics. In other words, a popular-based, multi-faceted revolutionary movement is the basic prerequisite for a successful armed insurrection in Latin America. This type of multifaceted movement is of course far more difficult to organize than a small guerrilla force in a relatively isolated rural area, but it is not outside the realm of possibility, and it seems to be the only alternative. In fact, this type of revolutionary movement, referred to as the *brazo armado*, is now being considered in certain leftist circles in Latin America. It seems that, for them at least, the failure of Che's guerrilla operation in Bolivia has indeed been a rich source of experience upon which to build a new revolutionary theory.

As the preceding discussion attempts to make clear, Che did indeed fail in the short run. However, this short-run failure has forced many of the revolutionary elements in Latin America to engage in a thoroughgoing reappraisal of their strategies for gaining power. Moreover, as a result of his death, Che has become an important symbol of revolutionary courage and commitment throughout Latin America and elsewhere, and his example appears to have inspired a whole new generation of young revolutionaries to take up the struggle where he left off. As a result, Che's own words, taken from a passage in his essay "Guerrilla Warfare: A Method," seem to suggest an answer to the question concerning the long-range significance of his defeat in Bolivia: "The outcome of today's struggles is not important. As far as the final result is concerned, it does not matter whether one movement or another is temporarily defeated. What is decisive is the determination to struggle, which is maturing every day, the awareness of the necessity for revolutionary change, and the certainty that it is a possibility."

Perhaps the present situation can best be compared with the aftermath of the disaster suffered by Castro and his young comrades when they stormed the Moncada barracks in 1953. After the Moncada disaster, Castro did not reject armed insurrection as the means to overthrow the Batista regime. On the contrary, he and his comrades turned defeat into victory through the development of a new strategy for carrying on the armed struggle. This seems to be what is taking place in Latin America today following the failure of Che's guerrilla operation in Bolivia. When and where a major new revolutionary effort will be made cannot be predicted, but the fact that it will occur seems to be almost a certainty, and when it does, the death of a revolutionary in a dusty little town in Bolivia will have been partially responsible for its occurrence.

Index